LED ZEPPELIN

LED ZEPPELIN

SONG BY SONG

JOHN VAN DER KISTE

FONTHILL

Fonthill Media Language Policy

Fonthill Media publishes in the international English language market. One language edition is published worldwide. As there are minor differences in spelling and presentation, especially with regard to American English and British English, a policy is necessary to define which form of English to use. The Fonthill Policy is to use the form of English native to the author. John Van der Kiste was born and educated in England; therefore British English has been adopted in this publication.

Fonthill Media Limited
Fonthill Media LLC
www.fonthillmedia.com
office@fonthillmedia.com

First published in the United Kingdom and the United States of America 2018

British Library Cataloguing in Publication Data:
A catalogue record for this book is available from the British Library

ISBN 978-1-78155-726-6

Typeset in 10pt on 13pt Sabon
Printed and bound in England

Acknowledgements

Particular thanks are due to my old friends and ever-present sounding boards, Miles Tredinnick and Ian Herne, for the regular exchanges we enjoyed by email while I was writing the book; to Mick Dark, Brian Moore, Francis Jansen, Robert Pingel, Roberto, and Giapolo for supplying me with photographs and scans of rare material from their personal collections; to Phil Swern, for additional information; to my wife, Kim, for her support and encouragement in reading the material and, as a professional musician, firmly curbing some of my wilder linguistic excesses brought on by too many years of having read the weekly rock papers since my misspent youth.

Finally, I acknowledge my gratitude as ever to my editors at Fonthill Media, Jay Slater, Jamie Hardwick, and Josh Greenland, for their encouragement and help in seeing the book into print.

CONTENTS

Author's Note

Composing credits on Led Zeppelin albums, particularly the earlier releases, have often been revised since initial release. For contractual reasons, Robert Plant was not given any joint writing credits on the first album when it first appeared. Additionally, certain tracks from various albums were credited at the time to Jimmy Page and have subsequently been amended for copyright reasons. The track listings for each album in this book include the current attributions, followed by their playing times.

Introduction

Led Zeppelin sprang from the ashes of The Yardbirds, remembered for several Top 10 singles between 1965 and 1966, and for three of the most-revered British rock guitarists: Eric Clapton, Jeff Beck, and Jimmy Page. The latter stayed with the group until they split in 1968 (notwithstanding a low-key reformation by two original members in 1992), and was authorised by the departing members to form another group to fulfil previously-contracted dates in Scandinavia. He approached several others, including vocalist Terry Reid, bassists Jack Bruce from the shortly-to-disband Cream, Ronnie Wood from The Jeff Beck Group, and Ace Kefford from The Move, and drummers Aynsley Dunbar from John Mayall's Bluesbreakers and B. J. Wilson from Procol Harum. The choice came down to Robert Plant and John Bonham, vocalist and drummer, respectively, with two local groups in the Midlands, and former musical arranger John Paul Jones, with whom he had worked on various sessions, on bass guitar and keyboards. After a few rehearsals, they worked with P. J. Proby on his album *Three Week Hero*, played the gigs in Denmark, Norway, and Sweden as scheduled, and returned to England to make their first album together.

Comprising blues standards and original material quickly co-written by the group for playing onstage, with sessions financed by Page, the record was begun on 27 September and completed within nine days. After being served with a 'cease and desist' order by Chris Dreja, former bass guitarist with The Yardbirds, who had only let them bill themselves as The New Yardbirds for the tour, they needed a new name. Inspiration came from a suggestion that had allegedly been made by Keith Moon of The Who two years earlier, when he and bass guitarist John Entwistle had briefly considered joining forces with Page and Jeff Beck, saying the idea would go down like a lead balloon. From that, Page had developed the idea of Led Zeppelin (the first word spelt so people would not mispronounce it), and they played their first gig under the new moniker on 26 October 1968 at Bristol Boxing Club.

The following month, their manager, Peter Grant, secured a $143,000 advance contract from Atlantic Records, at that time an unprecedented deal for a new group. The label had previously specialised in mostly American jazz, soul and blues, and their signing Led Zeppelin on the strength of their burgeoning reputation without even hearing a note they had played was indicative of their intention to embrace the progressive blues rock market, and as far as possible, fill the vacuum left by the phenomenally popular Cream. This contract gave group and management complete freedom to decide when to tour, full control over the contents, packaging, and release dates of albums, and acknowledging their veto of issuing tracks as singles in Britain, an almost unheard-of strategy at the time.

After playing their first show as Led Zeppelin at Surrey University, Guildford, on 25 October, tour manager Richard Cole organised a debut North American tour to start at the end of the year. The first album was released in January 1969, and in Britain ten weeks later, reaching the Top 10 in both territories. At first, reviews of their albums, particularly in America, were mostly hostile. Yet sales of their albums and concert tickets soon proved they had a fan base that did not need to rely on praise from sceptical music journalists.

During the rest of 1969, they completed four tours in Britain and America and recorded a second album, mostly in various North American studios. *Led Zeppelin II* topped the charts on both sides of the Atlantic, as would all but one of the studio albums they subsequently released during the decade. It developed the mainly blues-rock style as laid down by its predecessor. Though they had singles chart success in America, with 'Whole Lotta Love' reaching No. 4 in the American *Billboard* chart, they continued to forbid the release of material on 45 rpm in England and on television appearances. By now, they were increasingly successful as a draw in larger American venues, with some concerts lasting four hours or more, featuring expanded versions of their repertoire in which they often integrated verses and choruses from old blues, pop, and rock 'n' roll standards.

Much of the material on the first two albums was developed from extended jams based on blues standards and occasionally folk songs, resulting in a mix of musical and lyrical elements of different songs and versions, and improvised passages, to create new material. This would sometimes lead to accusations of plagiarism, and copyright disputes.

Although there had always been light and shade on their first two albums, for the third, the group explored their acoustic roots more deeply. After returning from an American tour, in 1970 Page and Plant went to stay at Bron-Yr-Aur, a remote Welsh countryside cottage without running water or electricity, to work on new material. The result was a softer, more folk-influenced set that initially sold as fast as ever, although sales soon tailed off.

Despite Atlantic Records trying to persuade them otherwise, they deliberately decided they would not give their fourth album a title, even insisting on a sleeve design that included no catalogue number or group name, with such details being confined solely to the label on the record inside. Perversely, the record variously known as '*Led Zeppelin IV*' (the obvious name), '*Untitled*', '*Four Symbols*', '*Zoso*' (after the members' group symbols printed on the inner sleeve), or '*Runes*' became their best-selling album ever, its success sealed by the presence of the evergreen 'Stairway to Heaven'.

The album's release was followed by extensive touring. These were the years of record-breaking achievements such as a North American concert tour in which they played at Tampa Stadium, Florida, one night to 56,800 fans, a number of which other acts could have only dreamed at the height of their success, and less happily performed three sold-out shows at Madison Square Garden, after which $180,000 of their proceeds from gate receipts were stolen from a safe deposit box in their hotel. At the same time, their travelling in a private jet airliner, *The Starship*, and ever more ambitious stage shows with new light shows, mirror balls, and lasers, went hand in hand with allegations of hedonism and excess, tales of groupies and debauchery, and destruction of hotel rooms and suites. While some wild behaviour doubtless ensued, gossip invariably breeds exaggeration, with tales often embroidered by journalists who were never there.

Even so, the pressure and exhaustion of lengthy tours and too much time spent away from his family at short notice were almost becoming too much for Jones. In 1973, he seriously considered leaving the group he had joined, initially thinking they would have an active life of only two or three years, after which he could retire to a more settled freelance musical career. A tongue-in-cheek comment to a journalist that he was to become choirmaster at Winchester Cathedral went into print and was taken at face value, until he put the record straight. To accommodate him, Grant agreed to make changes, such as more warning of schedules and less touring in school holidays, allowing him to spend more time at home with his wife and children.

Between tours, they recorded a fifth album, the first with a 'proper' title, *Houses of the Holy*, released in 1973. It did, however, continue a tradition of deliberately omitting their name and album title from the sleeve.

During a break from touring in 1974, group and management launched their own record label, Swan Song, after the five-year deal with Atlantic Records expired, although the parent company still distributed all products. Their next release in February 1975 was a double album, *Physical Graffiti*, containing material recorded at various sessions over the previous three years. Its star track was the oriental-sounding 'Kashmir', regarded by some as their finest-ever achievement.

After a further tour of North America covering January to March 1975 and five sold-out dates at Earl's Court Arena, London, in May, they scheduled further dates in North America, Europe, and the Far East from August onwards. It was cancelled when Plant and his wife, Maureen, were seriously injured in a car accident while holidaying on the island of Rhodes in Greece earlier that month. While they were recuperating, the group wrote and recorded another album. *Presence*, released in March 1976, saw a slight change from their experiments in acoustic and world music to a greater reliance on guitar jamming. The continued sabbatical from touring forced on them during Plant's recovery allowed them to complete a concert film, *The Song Remains the Same*, based around the Madison Square Garden gigs in July 1973, with out-of-concert fantasy sequences involving each member and an accompanying soundtrack double album. Promoted as their way of giving fans 'a personal and private tour of Led Zeppelin', film and album were released in October. Grant later called it 'the most expensive home movie ever made', but despite a muted reception from the press, particularly in Britain where their tax exile status had prompted some adverse criticism, it performed well at the box office and came out on video and then DVD.

On the long-postponed next American tour, the most successful show was one at the Silverdome, Pontiac, Michigan, on 30 April 1977, where they set another attendance record with an audience of 76,229, the largest figure to that date for a single act show. Nevertheless, the whole project was beset with problems and curtailed by tragedy. Other dates were marred by fans trying to gatecrash venues or gain entry by throwing bottles and rocks through glass doors, and a riot ensued after one gig was cut short because of a severe thunderstorm. After playing at the Oakland Coliseum, California, on 23 July, Bonham and some of the group's support staff were arrested following an incident when a member of promoter Bill Graham's entourage was badly beaten up after an argument. Their second concert at the venue the next day would be their last live appearance in the United States ever. A devastating blow followed that week on their arrival at a hotel for a show at Louisiana, when Plant took a call to say that his five-year-old son, Karac, had been taken ill with a stomach virus and just died. The rest of the tour was immediately cancelled.

After time off to allow the grief-stricken vocalist time to recover, in the autumn of 1978, they held rehearsals in London and went to work at Polar Studios, Stockholm, owned by two members of ABBA and their manager, Stig Anderson. The world-weary group's difficulties over the previous two or three years had been exacerbated by Page's increasing dependency on heroin and Bonham's alcoholism. *In Through the Out Door*, the resulting album, recorded in three weeks, thus relied heavily on the input of Plant and Jones, with the latter remarking that they were in two distinct camps by then, he and Plant 'in the relatively clean one'. Their strength as a songwriting partnership had blossomed with the vocalist's lyrics becoming more personal, even autobiographical, while Jones, whose talents as a tunesmith had not always been fully exploited, was experimenting more with his newly acquired Yamaha GX-1 synthesiser. Both would arrive earlier in the studio to start working and rehearsing immediately so they had songs ready before Page and Bonham had even arrived. Two of the seven songs on the album were credited to Plant and Jones alone—the only original Led Zeppelin tracks that Page had no hand in writing.

Their tax exile status had prevented them from touring Britain, and in their view, trying to get back into the public eye at home was like 'trying to get in through the "out" door'. Those last five words gave them the title of yet another album that topped the charts on both sides of the Atlantic on release in August 1979. In America, during two weeks in October and November, their entire catalogue returned to the *Billboard* Top 200.

Meanwhile, in August, the group had resumed live work in Europe. After two shows in Copenhagen, close to where they had made their on-stage debut nearly eleven years before, in England, they headlined two concerts at the Knebworth Music Festival, playing to a rapturous crowd of about 104,000 on the first night.

Plant was reluctant to tour America again, and the group wanted to avoid some of the negative press attention they had experienced in Britain. Grant therefore arranged a short European tour in the summer of 1980 with dates in West Germany, Austria, Belgium, the Netherlands, and Switzerland, hoping to rekindle the vocalist's enthusiasm for a return across the Atlantic. They played medium-sized to small venues with more modest stages and lighting and shorter sets, generally lasting about two hours. Two dates had to be cut short. At the Stadthalle, Vienna, on 26 June, Page was hit in the face by a firecracker thrown from the audience, and there was a delay before they finished the show. One night later at the Messezentrum Halle, Nuremberg, Bonham collapsed after the third number and was rushed to hospital, the rest of the group claiming that he had probably overeaten. He recovered in time for the rest of the tour, winding up at Eissporthalle an des Jaffestraffe on 7 July with 'Whole Lotta Love' as the final encore.

Rehearsals were then scheduled for their first North American tour for three years, due to open on 17 October. On 24 September, Bonham was picked up by one of their assistants, Rex King, to meet the others at a studio near Maidenhead. He drank heavily for much of the day, and after finishing, they returned to Page's house at Windsor. Having fallen asleep during the evening, Bonham was put to bed just after midnight and laid on his side. On the following afternoon, he was found dead. An inquest returned a verdict of accidental death, the cause being asphyxiation from his own vomit.

Rumours that the others intended to replace him, either with Simon Kirke (the Bad Company and Free drummer who had joined them on stage on two of the German dates in July), Bev Bevan, Cozy Powell, Barriemore Barlow, or Carmine Appice, were mere speculation. Without him, they had no heart to carry on and the tour was cancelled. On 4 December, they issued a statement saying that 'the loss of our dear friend, and the deep sense of undivided harmony felt by ourselves and our manager, have led us to decide that we could not continue as we were'.

In November 1982, *Coda*, featuring eight previously unreleased tracks spanning their entire career, reached the shops. Page explained that the main reason for issuing it was because of the popularity of bootleg material, showing there was still an appetite for studio outtakes. It later emerged that it was also to honour existing contractual commitments to Atlantic, and to cover tax demands on previous monies earned.

Over the next few years, Plant, Page, and Jones all continued to pursue musical careers on record and stage, remaining active in the recording industry, undertaking solo projects and collaborations with others—occasionally each other. Plant has been by far the most prolific as a soloist and fronting various new groups, among them The Honeydrippers with Page and Jeff Beck, The Priory of Brion, Strange Sensation, Band of Joy (the same name as that of his original pre-Zeppelin outfit), and, most recently, The Sensational Space Shifters, as well as a partnership with Alison Krauss. Page has teamed up with Paul Rodgers and other musicians for two albums as The Firm, with David Coverdale for one, Roy Harper for another (regarded as a Harper album featuring Page on guitar), and with The Black Crowes on yet another, *Live at the Greek: Excess all Areas*, recorded at the Greek Theatre, Los Angeles, featuring several Zeppelin numbers. Jones's output has included a soundtrack, an instrumental, and a vocal album, plus a collaboration with Diamanda Galas and another as part of the supergroup Them Crooked Vultures.

The next reappearance on stage of all surviving members together was for the Live Aid concert on 13–14 July 1985 at JFK Stadium, Philadelphia, with a fifteen-minute set comprising 'Rock and Roll', 'Whole Lotta Love', and 'Stairway to Heaven', featuring Jones playing keyboards, bass guitarist Paul Martinez, and drummers Phil Collins and Tony Thompson. With badly functioning monitors, lack of rehearsal, Page's out of tune guitar, and Plant's hoarseness after singing at three gigs on the trot beforehand, it was not their finest moment. Another unsatisfactory regrouping took place on 14 May 1988 for the Atlantic Records fortieth anniversary concert at Madison Square Garden, New York, when Bonham's son, Jason, played drums. There was a more informal reunion in April 1990 when Jason was married at Kidderminster, and the three members of his father's group joined him for a jam at the reception.

Accompanied by additional musicians, Page and Plant were reunited in 1994 for an MTV show, *Unledded*, with reworked songs from their back catalogue, album *No Quarter*, and a world tour. The song 'No Quarter' had been largely Jones' work, and he was annoyed at not being informed of the collaboration in advance. Page and Plant continued to work together with a group (ironically featuring another bassist called Jones, first name Charlie—Plant's son-in-law, married to his daughter, Carmen) on an album of new material, *Walking into Clarksdale*, released in 1998. Times had changed: a single from the album, 'Most High', reached the British Top 30, and that same week, they promoted it on BBC's *Top of the Pops*.

Meanwhile, the albums continued to sell, aided by compilations, remasterings, and box sets, plus a compilation, *BBC Sessions*, in 1997 (reissued with a third disc of additional material in 2016) and a lengthy live set, *How the West was Won*, in 2003, all overseen by Page. As for reunions, the three surviving members plus Jason Bonham got it right at a tribute concert for Atlantic Records co-founder Ahmet Ertegun, who had died the previous year. Twenty million applications for tickets were made online for the show at the O2 Arena, London, on 10 December 2007. *Celebration Day*, a film of the show, was released in various audio and video formats five years later. It had gone so well that there was immediate speculation about a lasting reunion, but Plant was reluctant to shelve his other commitments, and after a few months of speculation, he confirmed that he did not intend to have any role in a more permanent reincarnation. Page and Jones considered a few alternative replacements, notably Steven Tyler of Aerosmith, but by January 2009, they announced that the idea would go no further.

Initially regarded as a blues group who almost single-handedly created hard rock or heavy metal, they soon proved themselves more eclectic than most of their peers. From the first album onwards, they had also drawn on elements of folk and country, and subsequent records ventured into rock 'n' roll, psychedelia, soul, funk, jazz, reggae, and eastern music. Far from staying with the standard pop music lyrical preoccupations of love and romance (or lust), they later incorporated elements of mysticism and mythology into their subject matter, a result of Plant's interest in history, literature, and folk legends. With Page's interest in the occult, there were accusations that their records were strewn with subliminal satanic messages, something they readily dismissed as nonsense.

Having been the butt of critics and of general disapproval by most people outside their ardent fanbase for so long, it came as some surprise to them in the new millennium to realise that their music had stood the test of time, and they were highly loved and respected after all. Plant commented in an interview in 2003 that it seemed strange that they could be reviled in several generations, and then find out that they were people's favourite group: 'We were considered underground, and I've got band members whose parents wouldn't let them listen to us; they thought it was the devil's music'.[1]

In 2014, it was confirmed that they were the second highest-selling group ever, again bested by the Fab Four. They were responsible for a major change in the music industry at the start of the 1970s by leading the way in the development of album-orientated rock (AOR) and stadium rock, how music was sold and heard on records, radio and concerts, and being broadcast regularly without the benefit of Top 40 singles playing, and selling out major shows at arenas worldwide without support acts. All in all, they are arguably second only to The Beatles as the most influential rock group of all time.

1

Led Zeppelin

UK: released 28 March 1969, Atlantic, No. 6 (2014 reissue, No. 7)
US: released 12 January 1969, Atlantic, No. 10 (2014 reissue, No. 7)
Current edition: Atlantic CD
Personnel: Robert Plant—lead vocals, harmonica
Jimmy Page—acoustic, electric and pedal steel guitars, backing vocals
John Paul Jones—bass guitar, Hammond organ, backing vocals
John Bonham—drums, timpani, backing vocals
Viram Jasani—tabla (track 6)
Recorded at Olympic Studios, London, September–October 1968
Produced by Jimmy Page

Led Zeppelin's first album was recorded in thirty-six hours, at a total cost of £1,782. It featured material that was solidly rehearsed and played as the core of their Scandinavian tour just before they entered the studios. Four of the tracks last over six minutes each, built partly out of jamming old blues standards and folk material. This resulted in improvisation, inspiration, and borrowing from songs that, at the time, were assumed to be traditional and thus public domain, hence composing credits to Page, or 'traditional, arranged by Page', later corrected when legal action was threatened.

Plant received no songwriting credits on the initial release. The usual reason given is that he was still under contract to CBS Records, but according to Page, he was not 'contributing anything meaningful, either lyrically or musically' at first. His name was added to credits on reissues and remastered editions.

Lyrics were likewise often improvised, and sometimes slightly rewritten before final recording. While the influences of classic blues performers such as Muddy Waters, Skip James, and Willie Dixon were paramount, two of the tracks (one vocal, one instrumental) show a debt to folk musicians like Joan

Baez and Bert Jansch—Page being much under the spell of acoustic guitar styles and open tunings favoured by the latter. As for electric guitar, he used his Fender Telecaster on much of the album, except for a Gibson Flying V on 'You Shook Me'. Somebody was trying to sell him one at the time and he could not afford it (his financial situation would soon improve), but he asked to borrow it so he could try it out during the sessions.

The front cover design, chosen by Page, features a 1937 photo of the *Hindenburg* airship on fire, while the pictures of each member on the back were taken by Chris Dreja of The Yardbirds.

A remastered version was issued in June 2014 in six formats, a standard CD edition, deluxe two-CD edition, standard LP version, deluxe three-LP version, super deluxe two CD plus three LP version with a hardback book, and as high-resolution 96k/24-bit digital downloads. The deluxe and super deluxe editions include bonus material from a concert at Olympia, Paris, recorded in October 1969.

Tracks

1. 'Good Times Bad Times' (Page, Jones, Bonham, Plant) 2.46

Track one in the Led Zeppelin catalogue opens with short guitar fragments and a swift quote on the drums before Plant's vocals, double-tracked throughout most of the song, and Jones is given the field for a very short bass run immediately after two of the choruses. He once said that usually anything played by the group with lots of notes was his, 'and anything with chunky chords was Page's. Things like "Good Times Bad Times", those are my sort of riffs, they're quite busy.'[1]

Page played his Fender Telecaster through a Leslie speaker, a device regularly used by The Beatles in the studio on their later work from the *Revolver* album onwards that modified the sound by rotating the loudspeakers to create a special effect for the solo, and placed microphones all over the recording studio to capture a live feel. Bonham used a triplet on his bass drum to sound like two bass drums, using the tip of his toe to flick the bass pedal back quickly. Speaking about how the song and whole sound came together, Page later recalled that it developed from a riff 'with a great deal of John Paul Jones on bass, and it really knocked everybody sideways when they heard the bass drum pattern, because I think everyone was laying bets that Bonzo was using two bass drums, but he only had one.'[2]

Almost deceptively mainstream pop/rock, it is one of three numbers on the album well shy of three minutes in length. It was released as a single in America, where it reached No. 80, and other overseas territories including Canada, Japan, and Netherlands, making the Top 20.

Despite its short length, it was rarely featured on stage in full. On early dates, it was sometimes used as an introduction to 'Communication Breakdown', in medleys with the same song when Jones also played a bass solo, and with 'Whole Lotta Love'. After being laid to rest from 1972 for the remainder of their career, it was revived as the opening song for their reunion show at the O2 Arena, London, in November 2007. Jones remarked afterwards to a journalist that it was the hardest riff he had ever written, and the most difficult to play.

2. 'Babe I'm Gonna Leave You' (Anne Bredon, Page, Plant) 6.42

This folk song was written by Anne Bredon, then known as Anne Johanssen, in the 1950s. It became widely known not through a recording, but through the guest appearances of herself and another folk singer, when they sang it live on the American radio show *Midnight Special*. Unfortunately, she had never registered it with ASCAP (American Society of Composers, Authors and Publishers). It subsequently came to the notice of Joan Baez in 1962, who included a performance on a live album, crediting it as 'traditional'. At least three other versions appeared on record during the next three years. The first, in 1964, was the B-side of the only single by British group The Plebs, a RnB shuffle similar in style to early Kinks and Small Faces, credited 'Traditional, arranged by Chris Dennis', their keyboard player. In 1965, The Association, who would share a bill with The Yardbirds at the University of Massachusetts on 6 April 1968, released a slower version more in keeping with the song's folk origins as a single only in America, crediting Bredon as the writer (full marks to them for being the first to get it right), while in Britain, Mark Wynter's heavily orchestrated ballad version, with American folksinger Janet Smith given the composing credit, appeared on a 45 in Britain.

Page had always loved the song, and later said that he had worked out the arrangement during his time as a session guitarist, 'sitting in the darkness playing my six-string behind Marianne Faithfull'.[3] It was one of the numbers he played Plant at their first meeting together in July 1968 and earmarked for any future collaboration.

On initial release, the group credited it as 'traditional, arranged by Page'. After Bredon was made aware of their version and paid substantial royalties, the writing credits were altered as above, acknowledging Plant's contribution towards improvising the new lyrics. Numerous other acts have since recorded it as well, among them Quicksilver Messenger Service, Man, and Miley Cyrus. Most of the more recent versions listed online on Allmusic credit Paul Bennett and Edward Darling alongside Bredon as co-writers, with a few adding the names of Page and Plant as well.

There is speculation that Page had previously recorded the song with Steve Winwood in the late summer or early autumn of 1968, on a widely circulated bootleg tape. It is more probably a group try-out on which the organ was played by Jones rather than the front man of Traffic.

The group's version is a remarkable fusion of acoustic folk and hard rock, the extreme rapid dynamic contrasts that Page had said he was aiming for. For the first minute, it features just acoustic guitar and a gentle vocal, until drums join in behind a spirited sequence of electric guitar chords for about ten seconds. It reverts to the restrained vocal and acoustic guitar for another forty seconds or so, until Plant's voice takes flight into a Janis Joplin-style scream, reminiscent of the powerful version of George Gershwin's 'Summertime' that Joplin had recently recorded with Big Brother & The Holding Company on their second album *Cheap Thrills*. About two minutes in, there are some atmospheric ascending sound effects, after which the group launch into a much louder passage dominated by a riff based around five descending notes, as frequently used by others since—notably by Chicago on their 1970 hit '25 or 6 to 4'. The remaining four and a half minutes alternate between passages with Plant's restrained vocal against Page's delicate acoustic picking, and a dramatic heartfelt screaming vocal with more punchy chords, pounding drums, and a brief burst of electric guitar. During the last forty seconds, it comes to a graceful conclusion as Plant slowed down to the final line 'that's when it's calling me back home', followed by a delicate guitar picking coda.

As Page commented, although the group were heavily involved in what he called 'a sort of progressive blues thing', one of the most important parts was the acoustic input. This song with the flamenco additions, he said, was a good example. 'The drama of it—the light and shade—I don't think had been touched by anybody'.[4]

It was featured by the group on stage throughout their 1969 concerts, and then rested until Page and Plant brought it back on the shows during their 1998 reunion. Plant has since featured it on tours as a solo artist, and with his groups Strange Sensation and The Sensational Space Shifters.

3. 'You Shook Me' (Willie Dixon, J. B. Lenoir) 6.28

First recorded in 1962 by Muddy Waters, it was later popularized by the Jeff Beck Group, whose vocalist at the time was Rod Stewart. They recorded it on their album *Truth*, released in August 1968, with Jones playing organ on the session. Their version lasted only two and a half minutes, while Led Zeppelin's extended to more than twice that length. Beck and Stewart later complained that Page had 'stolen' their idea, particularly as he and Grant had followed the Jeff Beck Group around and seen several of their gigs earlier that year, but Page insisted that it was down to coincidence, similar background, and tastes. Waters heard their recording the following year and reportedly loved it.

Although the group's version sounds like it was more improvised, it had been tightly arranged beforehand, from Page's opening notes on electric guitar and Plant's harmonica solo to the steady rhythm section throughout. Two minutes in, Jones contributes an organ solo, using the pedals for bass, with considerably more freedom than he was allowed on the one by Beck, which flows smoothly into harmonica and then guitar. This is where the borrowed Gibson Flying V was used. With the big humbuckers (pickups), he said, 'it was so powerful you can hear it breaking up the amp in the middle of the song. I could've tidied it up, but I really liked hearing the amp really struggle to get the sound out. It's really fighting through the electronics to get out of that speaker'.[5]

Five minutes in, the final verse begins, giving way after forty seconds to the remarkable call-and-respond between guitar and vocal, matching each other note for note to perfection. This was achieved partly by Page's use of reverse echo, which involved manipulating a recorded echo so it preceded the main sound instead of following it, something he had originally developed when recording one of the last Yardbirds' singles. When he told the engineer, Glyn Johns, what he wanted to do, Johns said it would not be possible. As the producer, Page insisted, especially as he knew from previous experience that it would work. A concise guitar solo brings the song to a swift conclusion. The music then continues without a break into the next song.

It was a regular favourite on their early tours until autumn 1969, and thereafter used in part on some of their medleys, particularly with 'How Many More Times'. Page later played it with The Black Crowes on *Live at the Greek*.

4. 'Dazed and Confused' (Page, inspired by Jake Holmes) 6.28

The Yardbirds had headlined a show in New York City in August 1967 at which singer-songwriter Jake Holmes was one of the support acts. They were so impressed with this song—about a bad acid trip—that Page and drummer Jim McCarty bought their own copies of his album, and they then 'rewrote and rearranged the song' based on the descending bassline riff, retaining most of the lyrics but improvising a few additional lines. Holmes had written the song a few months before playing his show with The Yardbirds, and did not become aware until much later that the group had adapted it and claimed it as their own. At first, he was reluctant to take them to court as he did not want to spend a large amount of money on a case which might have failed. In 2010, he decided to act, motivated largely by a favourable judgment for organist Matthew Fisher in a similar case concerning Procol Harum's 'A Whiter Shade of Pale' in which he claimed official recognition as co-writer, thus setting a precedent that songwriting credits claimed by others could be challenged in a British court many years retrospectively. Holmes reached an out-of-court settlement in November 2011 with Page and the credit was accordingly altered as above. All he wanted, he said, was a fair deal. Page had taken his song 'and put it in a direction that I would never have taken it, and it became very successful. So why should I complain? But give me at least half credit on it.'[6]

The group's version opens with a few seconds of Jones's descending bass riff, joined by Page's guitar played with a violin bow, a technique that had been suggested to him during his session work years before by violinist and orchestra leader David McCallum. Plant's vocal enters about fifteen seconds in and the drums come in another twenty-five seconds after that. The slow haunting pace is maintained for around three minutes, with the bowed guitar providing an eerie mood while the bass and drums provide a suitable backdrop. Around three minutes and thirty seconds in, the drums and bass accelerate for a fast-paced guitar solo that features, to some extent, Plant echoing the notes. Five minutes in, it returns to the slow pace and riff on which it all began, coming to an orderly conclusion another ninety seconds after that.

It was featured on each concert tour up to and including the 1975 Earl's Court shows, generally including parts of one or more other numbers such as 'San Francisco (Be Sure To Wear Some Flowers In Your Hair)', 'Spanish Eyes', and 'Woodstock', and lasting up to thirty minutes. Thereafter, Page retained parts of the bowed guitar passage as the intro to 'Achilles' Last Stand' on the 1977 tour, and 'In the Evening' on the Knebworth 1979 shows and European dates the following year. On *Celebration Day*, the album of the O2 Arena show, it manages to be the longest of all sixteen tracks, at eleven minutes and forty-five seconds in duration.

5. 'Your Time is Gonna Come' (Page, Jones, Plant) 4.34

The warm sounds of a church organ, reminiscent of some early Procol Harum classics, dominate the first minute of this fairly slow song, appropriately from a musician who as a boy regularly played the organ in church. Only after the first sixty seconds do drums, bass, and acoustic guitar come in, just prior to the opening verse, a rather misogynistic lyric addressed by an aggrieved cheated-on lover to a girl who has been 'messing around with every guy in town'. Some lyrics bear a resemblance to those in the first verse of Ray Charles's 'I Believe to my Soul'. The organ reappears on the gospel-like chorus—or, more accurately, the title phrase sung four times, backing vocals courtesy of Bonham, Jones, and Page. The second verse features Page adding some Fender ten-string steel guitar (by his own admission, slightly out of tune) as well as acoustic. It became the first Led Zeppelin song to be covered by another artist, when Sandie Shaw included her own version on the album *Reviewing the Situation* a year later.

Coincidentally, around the time the album sessions were taking place, Joe Cocker's 'With a Little Help From My Friends', surely one of the most innovative and least commercial records to top the British chart in 1968, entered the Top 40. It featured a similarly eerie organ sound (the work of session musician Tommy Eyre), a similar build-up on the chorus, and Page on guitar in one of the last of his many sessions for other artists before forming the group. No less of a coincidence was that, shortly before he was asked to join Led Zeppelin, Bonham had been invited to play drums with Cocker's Grease Band but turned the offer down.

After playing it regularly in full on the 1968 Scandinavian tour, the group never featured it live again, apart from a segment as part of the 'Whole Lotta Love' medley, also including 'The Hunter', 'Rave On', and 'I'm a Man' on stage at the Budokan, Tokyo, on 24 September 1971, as recorded on a bootleg *Light and Shade*. Page later played it with The Black Crowes on *Live at the Greek*.

6. 'Black Mountain Side' (Page) 2.12

Led Zeppelin would later delve further and quite deeply into acoustic, folk, and roots music, but the influences had been there from the beginning, not only in covering a song they had heard from Joan Baez, but also in this crisp two-minute instrumental. It had been inspired by a traditional Irish folk song, 'Down by Blackwaterside', with Bert Jansch recording his own version on the album *Jack Orion*, released in 1966. His arrangement was learnt by Al Stewart, who taught it to Page when he was playing on the B-side of Stewart's first single. Nat Joseph, the founder of Jansch's label Transatlantic, sought legal advice, but as the melody was traditional, it would have been impossible for them to bring an action for plagiarism, despite Jansch's insistence that Page had 'ripped him off', or 'let's just say he *learned* from me'.[7] Joseph was advised that even if Jansch won an action against Page, there was the possibility that anybody else who had previously recorded the piece could sue on the grounds that 'Bert heard it from me'. Folksinger Anne Briggs, who had originally provided Jansch with the song, agreed on the grounds that 'borrowing and influencing' had always gone on, as it was how music developed through the ages. When people sang for pleasure and nobody received any money, such problems did not arise: 'It only becomes a very large philosophical question when money enters into it'.[8]

The recording features just Page on a borrowed Gibson J-200 acoustic guitar with both 'E' strings tuned down to 'D', and tabla drums played by Indian musician Viram Jasani.

Live performances usually featured it integrated into the middle of a longer instrumental, 'White Summer' (see p. 113), lasting around ten minutes or more. During the 1968–69 tour, a show at Spokane, Washington, featured 'Summer' on its own, and the combination of both was first played as part of their first-ever concert at the Fillmore West, San Francisco, on 10 January. On the 1980 European tour, 'Black Mountain Side' was used as an intro for 'Kashmir'.

7. 'Communication Breakdown' (Page, Jones, Bonham, Plant) 2.30

This short, sharp, simple, and almost punkish anthem for frustrated youth, just two minutes and thirty seconds long, takes a bow to Eddie Cochran's 'Nervous Breakdown', particularly in the guitar riff. The group were fervent admirers of Cochran, as testified to by regular performances of 'C'mon Everybody' and 'Somethin' Else' in their early live shows (see p. 121). It was one of the first songs Page and Robert Plant worked on together, developed from a riff that the guitarist worked out during the first tour in Scandinavia, when they were still billed as The New Yardbirds. The idea, Page explained, 'was to have a really raw hard hitting number. It's hard to describe the feeling of playing those numbers at the time, but it was so exciting and electrifying to be part of it, and one that was always so good to play, so staccato—just a knockout to do.'[9] When they came to recording, he played the guitar riff on his Fender Telecaster through a small, miked Supro amplifier throughout, using a fully closed Vox wah-wah pedal to create a 'guitar in a shoebox' sound on the lead, and added backing vocal towards the end of the song.

Punk, new wave, and new age of heavy metal groups would testify to the influence the song had on them. The 'downstroke riffing' that Page used (and which he admitted was difficult to play because of the constant, quick downstroke with the pick) particularly impressed Johnny Ramone, guitarist with The Ramones, while cover versions were later recorded by Iron Maiden, The Dickies, The Fleshtones, The Flaming Lips, and The Jeff Healey Band, among others. The sheer urgency of the sound and teenage angst of the lyrics was undoubtedly an influence on the class of '76–'77, no matter how much some of the punk rock audience would affect to despise Led Zeppelin by then. It had also inspired some of their contemporaries as well. Bassist Geezer Butler of Black Sabbath admitted that they listened over and over again to the first two Led Zeppelin albums, and their biggest hit, 'Paranoid', was an unashamed rip-off of 'Communication Breakdown'.

Atlantic pressed promotional copies as a single for release in Britain, but Grant and the group said no. It was, however, released as the B-side of 'Good Times Bad Times' in North America, several European countries, and Japan, and as an A-side in Costa Rica.

Always a live favourite, it was the only song to be included on the set list at every single gig they ever played. They often used it either to open shows or as an encore, and it was the last item they performed on stage at Earl's Court on their spring dates in 25 May 1975, and again at Knebworth in August

1979. The *BBC Sessions* compilation features three versions, all with slightly different improvisation each time, recorded within less than a fortnight in June 1969. The group were clearly devoted to the song and keen to experiment with it as much as possible.

It has lived on in the world of the large and small screen. In 1998, it was featured in the American sci-fi movie *Small Soldiers*, and eight years after that, it was in one episode of *The Simpsons*, 'G.I. (Annoyed Grunt)', when a group of soldiers are playing the guitar riff in a scene showing military recruitment.

8. 'I Can't Quit You Baby' (Willie Dixon) 4.42

A twelve-bar blues standard, this was first recorded by Otis Rush in 1956. The group's version follows a second one Rush made in 1966 fairly closely, a slow moody take quite close to the template they laid down on 'You Shook Me' and 'Dazed and Confused', with Plant and Bonham holding back at some moments but giving their all at others, while Page's solo incorporates a few seconds where he sustains a single note unaccompanied.

The song was a regular concert favourite for the first couple of years, with two versions from 1969 being included on *BBC Sessions*, and another from the Royal Albert Hall from 1970 appearing on the *Led Zeppelin* DVD in 2003 as well as an edited version on *Coda* (see p. 110). It was dropped from the set in 1970 and replaced with a similar slow blues, 'Since I've Been Loving You' (see p. 47). Part of it was integrated into the medley with 'Whole Lotta Love' during dates in 1972 and 1973. The surviving members of the group rehearsed but did not perform it at the Atlantic Records fortieth anniversary celebration concert in May. The song would be given a new lease of life in 2016 when covered by The Rolling Stones, with Eric Clapton on slide guitar, on their album *Lonesome and Blue*.

9. 'How Many More Times' (Page, Jones, Bonham, Plant) 8.28

At eight minutes and thirty seconds, this is the longest track on the album. Beginning with a hazy shuffle on bass guitar and drums, it is joined a few seconds in by bursts of guitar, partly using the violin bow and partly treated with echo. Page recalled experimenting with using the board to overdrive a Leslie cabinet for the main riff: 'It doesn't sound like a Leslie because I wasn't employing the rotating speakers. Surprisingly, that sound has real weight. The guitar is going through the board, then through an amp which was driving the Leslie cabinet. It was a very successful experiment'.[10]

Everything comes to a brief stop after three minutes and thirty seconds, then after a few seconds, tom-tom fills on the drums, bass, and bow effects return to create an almost ambient soundscape based around a two-note phrase and the tempo slows for a while (a similar pattern can be heard on the last part of the title track of Roxy Music's *For Your Pleasure*). The guitars and drums then build until joined by a bass run (later to be heard in the first few seconds of David Bowie's 'Jean Genie') that leads into a blues jam, parts of which came spontaneously to the group on the night of the recording session. It interpolates quotes from the spiritual 'Steal Away' and 'The Hunter', a blues number written by Booker T and the MGs and recorded by Albert King the previous year, before reverting to the original song and riff. The title and some of the vocals were inspired by 'How Many More Years' by Howlin' Wolf, written under his real name Chester Burnett. According to Page, the track was one of those made up of various little pieces from his Yardbirds days, 'played live in the studio with cues and nods'. Subsequent live performances would find them extending it by incorporating additional material, including quotes from Neil Young's 'On the Way Home' and John Lee Hooker's 'Boogie Chillin''.

On initial pressings of the album, the track listing on the back of the sleeve gave the time as three minutes and thirty seconds. This was Page's attempt to trick radio producers into playing it on air, and only realise too late that it was far longer than they thought.

It was a regular feature of their show when they used it as the closing number up to the end of 1970. During the instrumental section, Plant would give the three instrumentalists a brief showcase and thank the audience for coming. From then on, it was performed intermittently until the early stages of their 1975 American tour, when they brought it back in every concert as Page's injured finger temporarily prevented him from playing the more tricky 'Dazed and Confused' to his satisfaction.

2

Led Zeppelin II

UK: released 31 October 1969, Atlantic, No. 1 for one week (2014 reissue, No. 12)
US: released 22 October 1969, Atlantic, No. 1 for seven weeks
Current edition: Atlantic CD
Personnel: Robert Plant—lead vocals, harmonica
Jimmy Page—acoustic, electric and steel guitars, Theremin, backing vocals
John Paul Jones—bass guitar, organ, backing vocals
John Bonham—drums, timpani, backing vocals
Recorded at Olympic Studios, London; Morgan Studios, London; A & M, Quantum, Sunset, Mirror Sound, and Mystic Studios, Los Angeles; Ardent Studios, Memphis, Tennessee; A&R, Juggy Sound, Groove and Mayfair Studios, New York City; 'The Hut', Vancouver, April–August 1969
Produced by Jimmy Page

In the space of just under a year, the group recorded their second album over five months at several different studios in London and the United States in between a busy schedule of tour dates in Britain, Europe, and North America. Plant later recalled the frenetic pace during which they were writing numbers in hotel rooms, laying down a rhythm track in London, adding a vocal in New York, overdubbing harmonica in Vancouver, and then coming back to finish mixing at New York.

The nine tracks showed a few further experiments with more folksy, semi-acoustic material as well as heavy electric blues. Plant said that it was a definite step forward for them as they had improved on the first album with having been together for longer. The excitement was still there, and yet they could also play quieter material that was equally effective, as did groups like Fairport Convention. It also marked his emergence as a serious songwriter, as well as a certain honing of his vocal approach. He said that it was only during the sessions for the album that he started to feel at home as a vocalist in the studio with them. While they had recorded the first album, he had his doubts about remaining a long-term member of the group, felt uncomfortable because of the demands being made on him, and only gained confidence around the time they were making the second.

Page was also coming into his own as a producer, especially on the first and best-remembered track, with his innovative recording and drum miking effects, use of reverse echo, and a very small amp that he miked up effectively to help create a vivid picture in sound. An advertising campaign was built around the slogans 'Led Zeppelin—The Only Way to Fly' and 'Led Zeppelin II Now Flying'. It was the band's first album to hit No. 1 on both sides of the Atlantic and, if the deluxe 2014 reissue is included, the one that stayed on the British album charts longer than any of their others—129 weeks between 1969 and 2014.

The outer cover design was based on a First World War photograph of a German Air Force division with the faces of each member of the group, plus a few select heroes (thought to include Miles Davis and Blind Willie Johnson), airbrushed on from a 1969 publicity photograph, plus the outline of a Zeppelin on a brown background similar to the cover of the first album, thus giving the album the nickname of 'the Brown Bomber'. On the interior of the gatefold sleeve was a design that showed searchlights beaming down from a golden airship on to an acropolis-like structure, fronted by four columns like coffins, each one inscribed with the name of a member of the group.

The album was remastered and reissued in June 2014 in six formats: a standard CD edition, a deluxe two-CD edition, a standard LP version, a deluxe two-LP version, a super deluxe two-CD plus two-LP version with a hardback book, and as high-resolution 96k/24-bit digital downloads. The deluxe and super deluxe editions feature bonus material containing alternative takes, backing tracks, and the previously unreleased instrumental 'La La'.

Tracks

1. 'Whole Lotta Love' (Bonham, Willie Dixon, Jones, Page, Plant) 5.34

How, when, and where the riff of one of the group's most immediately recognisable anthems originated, nobody can agree. Page once said he came up with it in the summer of 1968 while playing guitar on his houseboat moored on the Thames in Pangbourne. At once, he knew it was strong enough to drive the entire song, rather than merely open it. After developing it further, he played it to the others while they were rehearsing for the Scandinavian tour and the first album, and the excitement was evident:

> I had a riff, everyone was at my house, and we kicked it from there. I had [the riff] worked out already before entering the studio. I had rehearsed it. And then all of that other stuff, sonic wave sound and all that, I built it up in the studio, and put effects on it and things, treatments.[1]

On another occasion, he was less specific: 'The riff came from me, but don't ask me where it came from before that, because it just came out of thin air, as nearly all riffs do'.[2] According to Jones, it probably came about from a stage improvisation during the band's playing of 'Dazed and Confused', while jamming on a Garnett Mimms number. Ask different people, get different answers.

The song was ready to add to the live set in the spring of 1969. In the studio, it was enhanced by the successful alliance with Page and engineer Eddie Kramer in the control room. As the huge drum sound was the foundation of the whole song, Page recorded it in a room at Olympic Studios with 28-foot ceilings. One of the assistant engineers, George Chkiantz, helped to achieve that sound by putting the drums on a platform and putting up microphones in unusual places, such as a stereo boom 8 feet above the kit, two distant side microphones, and another just 2 feet away from the bass drum. Page stated: '[My intention was] for the song to work as this panoramic audio experience, I needed Bonzo to really stand out, so that every stick stroke sounded clear and you could really feel them. If the drums were recorded just right, we could lay in everything else'.[3]

The riff is played on a Sunburst 1958 Les Paul Standard guitar. Eighty seconds in, for a passage lasting almost two minutes, it turns into a free almost jazz-like break involving a solo on Theremin—an electronic instrument consisting of a black box and antennae, originally used in the late 1920s to make mock-horror sound effects for early talkie films, and in the 1960s most famously by the Beach Boys on 'Good Vibrations', on which the sound is altered by moving the hand nearer to or further from the antennae. Page was inspired to use one by hearing Spirit, whom The Yardbirds had supported on tour, using one.

According to Kramer, the mix 'where everything is going bananas' was a combination of Page and himself on the console 'twiddling every knob they could lay their hands on'. Some of the effects were obtained by detuning the guitar and pulling on the strings, while others were on tape. Everything from slide guitar with backwards echo to sound effects simulating a napalm bomb explosion was included, while the engineer's 'knowledge of low-frequency oscillation helped complete the effect. If he hadn't known how to do that, I would have had to try for something else.'[4] Plant contributed by hitting the top end of his vocal range, uttering orgasmic moans in the freeform section. These were realistic enough to shock some more strait-laced American record programmers into thinking twice about playing the track, or else producing an edited version that omitted it. Coincidentally, No. 1 in the British singles chart for one week in October 1969—the month the album was released in America—was 'Je t'aime... moi non plus', banned by BBC radio and television stations and then withdrawn by the record company which initially released it (resulting in a speedy and very lucrative acquisition by another, less censorious company just two weeks before it topped the chart) for being too explicit and potentially offensive.

The foundation of the record was one of those classic three-note riffs that everybody wishes they had thought of first. In fact, somebody else had. The song was inspired and to some extent based on 'You Need Love', written by Willie Dixon and recorded by Muddy Waters in 1962. In 1985, Dixon brought a lawsuit against the group, settled out of court in his favour with an undisclosed payment and a joint writing credit on all subsequent reissues. Plant nonchalantly called it 'a nick, now happily paid for ... you only get caught when you're successful'.[5] The money went to a worthy cause, as Dixon used it to help launch an educational programme in America providing musical instruments for schools.

Steve Marriott also pointed out the similarities the song bore, not so much in the riff so much as in Plant's 'Woman—you need it' phrasing in the reverse echo section ninety seconds before the end, with which a song on the first Small Faces' album closed. Not only was Robert Plant a regular in the audience at their gigs in the Kidderminster and Stourbridge area, but whenever The Yardbirds and The Small Faces played a gig together, Page asked Marriott what the song was and he told him it was 'You Need Loving', 'a Muddy Waters thing', although on the group's first album, Marriott and bass guitarist Ronnie Lane claimed the writing credits between them. Keyboard player Ian McLagan, who was not credited, admitted it was 'a steal'. Page had always been an admirer of Marriott's style and had at one stage tried to headhunt him as vocalist for the group before approaching Plant, but was warned off by the Small Faces' manager Don Arden, who allegedly asked him how he would play guitar with ten broken fingers.

Did Led Zeppelin really plunder or plagiarise? The song may have borrowed from both Willie Dixon and the Small Faces, according to journalist Michael Hann, but it was not the same as either of its pieces of source material; what the group took, he argues, they transformed: 'They were derivative only in the sense that they took from existing forms; what they did with them created rock 'n' roll of a new form, one as at home with folk or blues or proto-metal'.[6] Page freely admitted that they did 'take some liberties', adding that it was Plant's fault as he was meant to change the lyrics but sometimes failed to do so. Plant's tongue-in-cheek response was that, when he said 'Hey, that's not our song', Page retorted, 'Shut up and keep walking'.[7] Other artists since then have readily taken the group's style as a blueprint for some of their work. On their 1987 Top 20 hit 'Still of the Night', Whitesnake's David Coverdale, sometimes dubbed by Robert Plant as 'David Coverversion', much to his irritation, bore more than a passing similarity to 'Whole Lotta Love' and a subsequent Zeppelin track, 'Black Dog' (see p. 55). Ironically, Coverdale later formed a brief musical partnership with Page.

When the album was released, American radio stations looked for a track that would fit their on-air formats with 'Whole Lotta Love' being the main contender. The album version lasted five minutes and thirty seconds, and some radio stations created their own edit lasting three minutes and twelve seconds, with the middle section removed, in order that young listeners' ears should not be corrupted by the mock-orgasmic section, and an earlier fadeout. Page was sent an acetate of the edit, and took exception to his lovingly-crafted work being mutilated in this way. On 7 November, Atlantic released the full version as a regular single in America, with 'Living Loving Maid (She's Just a Woman)' from the same LP as the B-side. An edited version was intended strictly for promotional release, but some such copies were released commercially in error. It reached No. 4 in America in January 1970, being certified gold for sales of 1 million copies three months later, and was also issued thus in France, Germany, Australia, Switzerland, Belgium, the Netherlands, Australia (where it reached No. 1), and Japan. Atlantic Records, UK, wanted the single available in any form, knowing—as has generally been the case—that singles and airplay stimulate album sales, but the group and Grant, pointing to the clause in their contract stipulating that they had final say, said no. Page was determined to block any release of an edited version, particularly one removing the section he had worked so hard in the studio to create.

Meanwhile in Britain, Polydor Records, which were at the time responsible for manufacturing and distributing all product on the Atlantic label, intended to issue the edited version in mono—very few singles in Britain being stereo before 1970. Radio 1 presenter Alan Freeman, an avid champion of the group from the start, played it regularly on the station's flagship Sunday afternoon BBC Radio 1 chart show *Pick of the Pops*, which, apart from an 'LP spot', rarely deviated from featuring anything but new and current chart 45s. Many listeners probably assumed that it was or soon would be available in that format as well as on the album. A release date of 5 December 1969 was scheduled, as confirmed by the existence of about 500 promotional copies sent to the music press and local newspapers with the date stamped by hand across the label, and about 500 stock copies for shops sent to a warehouse in Manchester for national distribution. Grant was also adamant on the 'no-singles' policy—public demand be damned—and ordered it to be withdrawn from sale. A few copies reached record shops, some being seized allegedly on personal visits by Grant or his employees for the purpose and destroyed along with the warehouse stocks, thus rapidly becoming collectors' items to exchange hands eventually at vast sums (collectors were warned to beware of counterfeit pressings). Some shops found it necessary to display counter posters advising customers that the record was not available as a single. Nevertheless, enough copies had already been sold across shop counters for it to reach No. 43 in the *Melody Maker* Top 50 for the week ending 20 December. By the time the next chart was published after the Christmas break two weeks later, it had dropped out after being officially withdrawn from sale, as confirmed by a letter from Polydor sent to all record dealers.

Not long before, Page had told the British music press that there was no reason why they should not try and record a good short track for 45 rpm release, citing Jethro Tull as an example of an album-oriented group who had proved 'that a good single can get through'. Teasingly, Grant later issued an official statement that they would go into the studios in December to record one after the completion of the current tour, but it never materialised. He later admitted it was 'a cover-up' and they never had any intention of doing so. The catalogue number allocated by Atlantic UK to the escaped 'Whole Lotta Love' copies, 584309, was therefore used for their next new release, 'Take It Off Him and Put It On Me', by Clarence Carter.

Former Yardbirds producer Mickie Most knew the song was a hit. Later in 1970, he, blues musician and singer Alexis Korner, and music arranger John Cameron formed a jazz-rock fusion outfit CCS ('Collective Consciousness Society') using the cream of British session musicians to record three albums and several singles between 1970 and 1974. Taken from their first LP, their largely instrumental version of 'Whole Lotta Love' became a No. 13 hit in Britain at the end of 1970 and also the theme music for *Top of the Pops*, the weekly BBC TV chart music programme, intermittently until the early 1980s. Page saw this as a mixed blessing: 'It was pretty infectious, I suppose, although its being on *Top of the Pops* every week killed it over here [in Britain], which was a drag'.[8] Almost three decades on, posterity delivered the verdict that it had succeeded in 'ameliorating the tune's sexual specificity without stripping it of its rutty throb … a playful, slithery token of generalised social sexiness—the perfect sonic emblem for a teenage pop show'.[9]

In 1997, two years after Grant's death, the remaining members of Led Zeppelin permitted the release of a three-track CD single featuring a four-minute and fifty-second edit of the song, plus 'Baby Come on Home' and 'Travelling Riverside Blues', to mark the reissue of their back catalogue at mid-price. Aided by TV exposure of a specially produced video featuring footage from the 1975 Earl's Court and 1979 Knebworth shows, it belatedly gave them their first ever appearance in the British singles chart that September for two weeks, entering at No. 21. Ten years later, after their one-off reformation for a concert at the O2 Arena, it came back into the chart as a download-only single for three weeks, with a peak position of No. 64 (see p. 63). At the same time, a small quantity of 45 rpm 7″ singles with an edited version on both sides was released for jukeboxes, as well as a 'Juke-Boxed Collector's Series' limited to 300 numbered 7″ copies, including an interview disc and a numbered certificate, with 'Juke-Boxed 003' on the spine of the box and on the barcode sticker.

In addition to CCS, many others have covered the song. One of the most regularly found versions on vinyl, notwithstanding its dubious quality, was a disco version in 1979 released on 12″ single and 7″ picture disc by Blonde on Blonde, alias *The Sun* page three models Jilly Johnson and Nina Carter, but it failed to chart. British dance combo Goldbug fared better with their arrangement in January 1996, which also sampled 'Asteroid', the Pearl and Dean cinema advertising company theme, entering the chart at No. 3. It was a major influence on Slash of Guns 'n' Roses, who commented that 'that introduction where the guitar comes in and then the bass and the drums and everything, was definitely the most primal and most sleazy, sexy kind of thing that I'd ever heard.'[10]

The song was naturally a regular part of their live show, with an American reviewer calling it one of the most effective concert numbers since the Rolling Stones' 'Honky Tonk Women'. From 1970 to 1973, it was usually the closing finale, including a rock 'n' roll medley, an encore with 'Black Dog' on the 1975 dates, and a medley encore with 'Rock and Roll' or, on one occasion, with 'Communication Breakdown' on the 1977 tour. In 1979 and 1980, it was played with a new arrangement, and perhaps appropriately was the last song they ever played live on their final gig in July 1980 in West Berlin. It was the second of the three songs performed at Live Aid in July 1985 by the surviving three with drummers Phil Collins and Tony Thompson, played again at the Atlantic Records anniversary in 1988 and at the O2 Arena show, both with drummer Jason Bonham.

In August 2008, Page gave another performance at the Olympic Games closing ceremonies in Beijing, with former *X Factor* winner Leona Lewis on vocals. Four years later, they both repeated the feat at the closing Olympic ceremonies in London. At Lewis's request, the line 'every inch of my love' was inappropriate for a female vocalist and therefore altered to 'every bit of my love'. Page said later that this appearance was his proudest musical achievement outside the group. Describing her performance as 'phenomenal', he said: 'It was a Led Zeppelin number but it took on another persona. I was proud to be able to play that riff for the handover'.[11]

2. 'What Is and What Should Never Be' (Page, Plant) 4.45

Beginning with Plant singing softly as the other instruments come in behind him, without changing tempo, it rocks out furiously after about twenty seconds. Throughout the remaining four minutes, it is a piece of contrasts, one moment soft, the next loud and challenging. It demonstrates his natural ability to go from almost a whisper to a scream in no time, his vocals phased and double-tracked during part of the verses.

It was one of the first songs recorded by the band for which he received a writing credit, with the lyrics for this song said to be about a romance between him and his wife's younger sister, and one of the first songs on which Page used his Gibson Les Paul guitar for recording. Just over three minutes in, for about five seconds, there is a wash of multi-tracked vocal harmonies bathed in echo, similar to the style that 10cc would later make their own on 'I'm Not in Love'. After that is a passage where there is clever use of stereo as start-and-stop guitar chords move between both channels, plus a section where the song stops briefly, starts again with a few stuttering guitar chords, and the sound of Bonham's Chinese gong.

Although it was regular fixture in the group's set list up to and including 1972, they rarely played it thereafter.

3. 'The Lemon Song' (Bonham, Chester Burnett ('Howlin' Wolf'), Jones, Page, Plant) 6.19

A return to the twelve-bar blues comes on this song inspired by, or equates to, a recast version of Howlin' Wolf's 'Killing Floor', a number that Jimi Hendrix had regularly played onstage in his early days, as well as one the group briefly featured during their first American tour. For the two subsequent American tours, the song evolved into 'The Lemon Song', with Plant often improvising lyrics on stage. The opening lyrics to both songs are actually identical. Twice in the song, firstly about ninety seconds in and then again about a minute before the end, there is a quickening of tempo, the cue for all three instrumentalists to cut loose, Page with some fierce chords and solo, Jones's busy bass, and Bonham driving the beat forward. The often-criticised lyrics, and the metaphor of 'squeeze (my lemon) till the juice runs down my leg' come from Robert Johnson's 'Traveling Riverside Blues', a song the group had recorded for a BBC session that year and would eventually appear on record, although Johnson took it himself from a song recorded earlier in 1937, 'She Squeezed My Lemon', by Arthur McKay.

In December 1972, Arc Music, owner of the publishing rights to Howlin' Wolf's songs, sued Led Zeppelin for copyright infringement on 'The Lemon Song', and the case was settled out of court. Though the amount was not disclosed, Chester Arthur Burnett (Howlin' Wolf's real name) received $45,123 from Arc Music immediately following the suit, and subsequent releases included a co-songwriter credit for him.

It was performed live regularly on the group's first three American concert tours, initially under the original title of 'Killing Floor'. In the 1971 Royal Albert Hall show, it was incorporated into 'How Many More Times'. Page played it with Plant while they were touring in 1995, and with The Black Crowes on *Live at the Greek*, while Plant joined Jack White of The White Stripes onstage to sing it when they were appearing at the Lollapalooza Festival, Buenos Aires, in March 2015.

4. 'Thank You' (Page, Plant) 4.49

This was the first Led Zeppelin song for which Plant wrote all the lyrics, as a tribute to his then-wife, Maureen. In the process, it became the one that made Page realise Plant could now handle writing the majority of the lyrics for the band's songs.

A mellow intro on twelve-string acoustic guitar and Hammond organ are joined by Plant's vocals, Page singing backing vocals on the bridge, beginning 'little drops of rain', an acoustic guitar break, and the occasional impassioned scream vocal from Plant all help to add colour. There are similarities between this and the Small Faces' power ballad 'Afterglow (Of Your Love)', with Plant's vocals sounding similar to those of Steve Marriott. After about four minutes, the song fades away softly on organ, and a few seconds later, it fades back in unobtrusively for a final crescendo.

It remained regularly in the group's set list until 1973, Jones using either organ or Mellotron. Plant performed part of it when he appeared at the Freddie Mercury tribute concert in London in April 1992, then segueing into Queen's 'Crazy Little Thing Called Love'. Two years later, Page and Plant revived it as part of their *Unledded* project and their world tours over the next two years. Plant featured it on his tour with Band of Joy in 2010–11. In the '90s, cover versions were recorded by Tori Amos and Duran Duran. It was also played at the funeral of Bonham's mother, Joan, in February 2011.

5. 'Heartbreaker' (Bonham, Jones, Page, Plant) 4.14

One of Page's armour-plated guitar riffs underpins the first couple of minutes behind Plant's vocal. After that comes a guitar solo with not only a change in the time signature, but also a different sound, even recorded in a different studio as an afterthought once the rest of the track had been completed; in Page's own words, it was 'sort of slotted in the middle'. After playing completely unaccompanied, with a hint of echo and then feedback at the end, the bass and drums return as the solo becomes more frenzied for the next fifty seconds. Finally, for the last thirty seconds, Plant reprises another verse and everything comes to a sudden stop mid-riff, then moving straight into the next track.

For Page, it was one of the album's high points: 'That song's pretty much in two sections—it stops and there's a whole guitar bit before it moves into the solo, like changing gears into overdrive'.[12]

It was a regular favourite on stage throughout the group's career and beyond. In 1971 and 1972, they opened most of their shows with 'Immigrant Song' segueing into 'Heartbreaker', and from 1973 onwards, the latter was often kept for the encore. Apart from 'Communication Breakdown', it was the only song they played live on stage every year from 1969 onwards. Page often used to add plenty of improvisation during his solo, and might include anything from Bach's 'Bourrée in E minor', from *Lute Suites*, as heard on the versions on *BBC Sessions* and *How the West Was Won*, to Paul Simon's 'The 59th Street Bridge Song (Feelin' Groovy)' and the traditional 'Greensleeves'. The 1973 Madison Square Garden's performance was included in the film of *The Song Remains the Same*, although omitted from the 1976 soundtrack album but restored on the remastered edition released in 2007. Their final performance of it was in Zürich on 29 June 1980. The surviving members and Jason Bonham played it at the Atlantic Records fortieth anniversary concert in 1988 at Madison Square Garden. Page played it on tour with The Black Crowes and on *Live at the Greek*.

6. 'Living Loving Maid (She's Just a Woman)' (Page, Plant) 2.39

Carrying on from the previous track without a break comes one of the group's most commercial numbers ever, almost unique in their catalogue in having a conventional pop chorus, and the only one on the album less than three minutes long. Page plays a Vox twelve-string, and he and Jones add backing vocals on parts of the title phrase throughout. If they really had a brisk, infectious, no-frills pop-rock tune of the right duration for a single at the time, this was it, and it actually found its place on a 45 as the B-side of 'Whole Lotta Love' in America. Supposedly written by a groupie who had been following Page around all summer, the cynicism in the lyrics is obvious: 'With a purple umbrella and a fifty-cent hat, Missus Cool rides around in her aged Cadillac'. It was mistitled 'Livin' Lovin' Wreck (She's a Woman)' on early British pressings.

Page said it was 'about a degenerate old woman trying desperately to be young', and it was among their songs that he disliked most.[13] They therefore never performed it on stage, though Plant revived it for a solo tour in 1990, singing it to a mock-Beach Boys arrangement.

7. 'Ramble On' (Page, Plant) 4.23

The album's most folk-like four minutes, this also marks the start of the group's association with mythological themes and psychedelia. The lyrics were inspired mainly by Plant's reading of the works of J. R. R. Tolkien, with the opening line 'Leaves are falling' a paraphrase of the first line of 'Namárië', a poem from the first volume of the trilogy, *The Fellowship of the Ring*, and references in a later verse to 'the darkest depths of Mordor' and 'Gollum and the evil one'. Musically, the song alternates between Plant singing gently to a backdrop of bass, drums (which on this occasion allegedly included Bonham playing a hard guitar case with his hands to get the right sound) and acoustic guitar, and a more intensive, almost screamed chorus, with the electric guitar cutting through loud and clear.

Part of it was performed in concerts in Canada shortly after the album's release, integrated into 'Babe I'm Gonna Leave You' one night at Toronto in November 1969 and into 'Communication Breakdown' at Vancouver in March 1970. It was only first played in full at the O2 Arena show in November 2007, and completed with a brief section of the bridge from 'What Is and What Should Never Be'. Page and Jones joined the Foo Fighters on stage at Wembley Stadium in June 2008 for another live performance of the number.

8. 'Moby Dick' (Bonham, Jones, Page) 4.20

Cream had thrown down the gauntlet on their first album with Ginger Baker's drum solo showcase, 'Toad', and it was inevitable that Bonham would rise to the challenge. This instrumental cut was based on recordings Page had made of him jamming in the studio and then edited together to make a single four-minute track. It features him drumming to a guitar riff structured around a twelve-bar blues pattern, based partly on the guitar on Bobby Parker's minor 1961 American hit 'Watch Your Step' and also on 'The Girl I Love She Got Long Black Wavy Hair', which they recorded for a BBC session in June 1969 (see p. 121). The riff comes to a halt about one minute in, leaving the field clear to Bonham beating out patterns on the drums and cymbals, with the riff returning for a swift thirty-second reprise at the end, pausing for a couple more drum fills before the grand finale. Part of the guitar section was used by BBC2 TV as the theme tune to its late night rock music show *Disco 2*, a forerunner of *The Old Grey Whistle Test*.

Bonham originally named it 'Pat's Delight', after his wife. According to her, it was later given the title 'Moby Dick' because their little son, Jason, kept asking him to play 'the long song', and when his father asked why, he replied, 'It's big like Moby'.

A regular feature of their live set from the American tour in October 1969 until their last tour of the country in summer 1977, the drum solo would sometimes last for up to half an hour, giving the other members a chance to leave the stage for a break after playing on the introduction. Sometimes Bonham dispensed with sticks, putting them aside or throwing them into the audience and continued playing with his bare hands. The version on *The Song Remains the Same*, recorded in 1973, is eleven minutes long, while the one on *How the West Was Won*, dating from the previous summer, clocks in at nineteen, with nothing but percussion to be heard for over sixteen minutes of them. That on the Led Zeppelin DVD of 2003, featuring the January 1970 Royal Albert Hall performance, is fifteen minutes long.

9. 'Bring It On Home' (Willie Dixon) 4.20

The album's final cut is a return to the Willie Dixon songbook, a song made famous by Sonny Boy Williamson, though originally credited to the group until Dixon's publishing company sued and again reached an out-of-court settlement for plagiarism as well as a reversion to his credit as a writer. Page later commented that only a very small amount was taken from Williamson's version and they merely threw it in as a tribute to him. A gentle start with a blues riff on bass behind Plant's harmonica and then vocals until one minute and fifty seconds in, after which it moves up a gear with a more funky beat, slashing guitar riff and Plant's vocal turning into a scream. Two minutes later, it comes to a brief halt and reverts to the more laid-back mode for the last thirty seconds, as harmonica dominates the other instruments to bring it to a graceful finish. Again, it sounds like two or more different numbers bolted together, partly as it was recorded in different studios.

It was frequently played live, initially as an encore on the 1970 British tour. Two years later, on their American dates in Los Angeles, as on *How the West Was Won*, it was performed as a medley with a middle section, 'Bring It On Back', credited to all four members as writers. This new middle section was retained as the intro to 'Black Dog' on the 1973 American tour. Although dropped thereafter, it resurfaced when the surviving members reformed with Jason Bonham at his wedding reception in 1990. Page and Plant brought it back on their world tours between 1995 and 1998, and Page played it on tour with the Black Crowes in 1999 and 2000.

Bonus Track

'La La' (Page) 4.10

An instrumental jam lasting four minutes, this was presumably a backing track waiting for some of Plant's lyrics but never reached that stage. The first fifty seconds is dominated by an uncharacteristically poppy, catchy three-chord riff on Jones's organ, with bass and drums in the background, sounding more like a bubble-gum tune from the likes of Ohio Express or 1910 Fruitgum Co. It then changes direction with a few crisp acoustic and electric guitar chords, taking on a heavier, more typically Zeppelin sound about ninety seconds in. Halfway through, the tempo changes, becoming slower and heavier, with some fiery wah-wah and slide guitar, and the organ reappearing shortly before the end.

3

Led Zeppelin III

UK: released 23 October 1970, Atlantic, No. 1 for four weeks (2014 reissue, No. 10)
US: released 5 October 1970, Atlantic, No. 1 for four weeks
Current edition: Atlantic CD
Personnel: Robert Plant—lead vocals, harmonica
Jimmy Page—acoustic, electric and pedal steel guitars, banjo, dulcimer, bass guitar (track 8), backing vocals
John Paul Jones—bass guitar, Hammond organ, Moog synthesizer, mandolin, double bass (track 9), string arrangements
John Bonham—drums, timpani, backing vocals
Recorded at Rolling Stones Mobile Studio, Headley Grange, Hampshire; Island Studios, London; Olympic Studios, London, May–August 1970
Produced by Jimmy Page

The group's third album had been written mostly by Page and Plant while staying at Bron-Yr-Aur in the spring of 1970. In the back-to-basics environment, they came up with several songs that demonstrated a greater emphasis on folk and acoustic sounds. After lodging in motel rooms while on tour, usually in America, they spent a couple of months away from it all in the depths of the countryside. They had soaked up the styles of guitarists such as John Fahey, Bert Jansch, and Davey Graham, and it paved the way for the more experimental work, which would be an increasingly important part of their *oeuvre* in future. Significantly, it was the only studio album by the group released in its vinyl form as a single album, which boasted no less than ten tracks (as opposed to seven, eight, or nine), five of which were less than four minutes long.

Page had always said he wanted music with light and shade, and the third album came with more than its predecessors. It marked a shift in the creative dynamics of the group, with the songwriting partnership of Plant as lyricist and Page as tunesmith dominating the next few albums, Jones and Bonham contributing at rehearsal or in the studio as material was shaped into the final product. All four members then convened at Headley Grange, a run-down property in East Hampshire, where they began recording on the Rolling Stones' Mobile Studio before adjourning to London to complete the process. Final mixing took place at Ardent Studios, Memphis, in August during the next American tour.

It astonished fans and critics who were expecting something similar to the previous two sets and found the more predominantly folksy Led Zeppelin an acquired taste. Page was staggered by the 'Led Zeppelin go acoustic' reaction from some sections of the music press, pointing out that there had been three mainly acoustic numbers on the first album and two on the second. Plant said that buyers were aggrieved by the lack of a 'Whole Lotta Love' Part 2 or anything like Black Sabbath's 'Paranoid'. In spite of lukewarm reviews and comparatively modest sales, the album's reputation has since soared as an innovative record that was doing far more than merely re-treading past glories. It was perhaps significantly their first album to enter the British chart at No. 1, enjoying four weeks (three consecutively and a return to the top after a week's break) at peak position. Their next six albums, including the live *The Song Remains the Same*, would all lead the list in Britain in the first or second week of release, but none would stay there for more than two weeks.

Other songs recorded at the sessions were released later, 'Hey, Hey, What Can I Do' on the B-side of 'Immigrant Song', a single in America and most overseas territories, on a 1972 compilation, and subsequently on the first box set (1990), and *Coda*, deluxe edition (2015); 'Bron-Yr-Aur' on *Physical Graffiti* (1975); and 'Poor Tom' on *Coda* (1982).

The cover and interior gatefold art showed a surreal collection of random images on a white background, mostly having a connection thematically with aviation. Behind the front cover is a volvelle or laminated card disc, covered with more images, including photos of the group members, rotated by hand to show through holes in the cover; moving an image into place behind one hole brings one or two others into place behind other holes.

The album was remastered and reissued in June 2014 in six formats: a standard CD edition, a deluxe two-CD edition, a standard LP version, a deluxe two-LP version, a super deluxe two-CD plus two-LP version with a hardback book, and as high-resolution 96k/24-bit digital downloads. The deluxe and super deluxe editions feature bonus material containing alternative takes, backing tracks, and the previously unreleased 'Bathroom Sound', 'Jennings Farm Blues', and 'Key To the Highway/Trouble in Mind'.

Tracks

1. 'Immigrant Song' (Page, Plant) 2.25

If fans had been expecting another 'Whole Lotta Love' on the third album, this exhilarating opening track surely came closest to it. It had been inspired by a visit to Reykjavik in June 1970 when they were invited by the Icelandic Government to come and play a concert in Reykjavik, but the day before they arrived, all the civil servants went on strike and the gig was going to be cancelled. The university staff and students therefore prepared a concert hall for them, and they were overwhelmed by the response from the audience. Six days later, back in England, they performed the song for the first time in concert during the Bath Festival of Blues and Progressive Music, where they were headlining in June.

After a faint count-in and a few seconds of hiss caused by feedback from an echo unit comes the pulsating riff and an introductory three-note 'A-ah-ahh-ah' from Plant, which as some listeners have pointed out, sounds just like a phrase in Rodgers & Hammerstein's 'Bali Ha'i', from the musical *South Pacific*. 'We come from the land of the ice and snow, from the midnight sun where the hot springs blow,' he sings in the opening line. His lyrics had been written from a perspective of Vikings rowing west from Scandinavia in search of new lands. Going to Iceland, he said, made them think of Vikings and big ships. Another phrase he used, 'The hammer of the gods', would become indelibly associated with the group, especially after the publication of Stephen Davis' biography of them, first published in 1985—albeit one with which the group were not very impressed. A galloping maelstrom of guitar, bass, and drums in unison powers the song throughout, with a couple of brief stops and restarts along the way, and at just over two minutes in length, there is no time for a solo—just a relentless wall of sound as Plant sings at full throttle of the men in earlier ages whose 'only goal will be the western shore', urged on by the cry of 'Valhalla, I am coming!' In a very mixed review, Lester Bangs of *Rolling Stone* singled out the track as one of the album's highlights for its 'bulldozer rhythms and Plant's double-tracked wordless vocal crossings echoing behind the main vocal like some cannibal chorus wailing in the infernal light of a savage fertility rite'.[1]

Just the right length for a single, it was released as such in America in November 1970, where it reached No. 16, and in several other countries across the world. The B-side, 'Hey, Hey, What Can I Do' (see p. 114), was the only non-album track the group released during their twelve years together. In Britain, its sole appearance during the age of vinyl was on a 1972 compilation album, *The New Age of Atlantic*. Initial Japanese copies included 'Out on the Tiles' on the B-side in error. Yet again, Atlantic hoped they could persuade group and management to release it as a British single, and an acetate was prepared, but it went no further.

Brian May once said he was 'the world's biggest Led Zeppelin fan', called them 'the blueprint', and admitted that Queen sometimes played 'The Immigrant Song' at their soundchecks 'just for the glory of the sound'. They performed it just once on stage—a short version lasting barely a minute, at Berlin during a tour of Europe in June 1986.

A regular opening number on concerts from 1970—including a solo by Page absent from the album version, which elongated it by about a minute—it is included as the first number on the concert recorded at the Paris Theatre for *BBC Sessions*. On the second half of the 1972 American tour, it was preceded by a short burst of music, 'LA Drone', added to heighten a sense of anticipation among the audience as the group were taking to the stage, as can be heard at the start of *How the West Was Won*. By 1973, it was occasionally being used as an encore before being dropped from the set altogether. When Jeff Beck was inducted into the Rock and Roll Hall of Fame in April 2009, Page presented him with the award and joined him on stage for an instrumental, which included part of 'Immigrant Song'. Beck and Page played the song together as part of the induction ceremony.

Although the group had long been reluctant to license their back catalogue for films, they agreed to its use in the comedy *School of Rock* (2003) and the superhero picture *Thor: Ragnarok* (2017). Mark Mothersbaugh, composer of the score to the latter as well as keyboard player and guitarist with Devo, had requested permission to enhance and update the original recording with a hundred-piece orchestra, but Page and Plant rejected it, insisting that the recording should not be altered. The jingle-friendly battle cry intro could also be heard at around the same time on a trailer for the Dave TV sci-fi comedy series *Red Dwarf*. A few years earlier, in 2011, a cover version by Trent Reznor, Atticus Ross, and Karen O was featured in the movie adaptation of *The Girl with the Dragon Tattoo*.

2. 'Friends' (Page, Plant) 3.55

This was where the group's fascination with Eastern-influenced music began. Looking back many years after recording it, Plant recalled that while growing up, he was soaking up the sounds and the diverse mix of music from nearby houses. He would walk up the alley between their terraced houses 'and just sit on the lino with my neighbours, have a bowl of curry, listening to their music. At the top of the street, at the Fox and Dogs, there was Caribbean music, too: you'd hear Alton Ellis, the Skatalites, Delroy Wilson'. It was gradually dawning on him around this time that there was 'something really splendid and other-worldly about trying to even touch those bigger ideas as a British rock group to go past the idiom of singing about bars and chicks and all that crap, which unfortunately is the *lingua franca* of popular song. There are other dynamics of life, and we started to recognise that here.'[2]

A few muffled seconds of chat and laughter introduce one of the few group's songs to include strings, arranged by Jones who also plays synthesiser (heard briefly but to good effect at the end) as well as bass guitar. Page uses an open-C6 chord (C-G-C-G-C-E) tuning on acoustic guitar, as well as twelve-string and an Altair Tube Limiter, an electronic device to enhance the acoustic quality of his Harmony guitar, while Bonham plays tabla drums. The combined effect evokes the sound of Indian classical music to the lyrics in which Plant sings of bonhomie towards one's fellow man and of how 'the greatest thing you ever can do now is trade a smile with someone who's blue now'. There are theories that it was inspired by an almighty row Page had just had with somebody, possibly a friend or a family member.

Predominantly a studio creation, it was quite a radical departure from the group's usual sound, with its overtones of groups like Crosby, Stills & Nash. The group only played it live once, at Festival Hall, Osaka, on one of the dates during their Japanese tour in September 1971. They re-recorded it the following year with the Bombay Symphony Orchestra on a visit to India, using tabla drums and sitars, and the result appeared on the 2015 remastering of *Coda* (see p. 116). An instrumental version, or more accurately the backing track, appears on the 2014 deluxe version of *Led Zeppelin III*.

It was among the songs revisited some two decades on by Page and Plant, accompanied by a Middle-Eastern orchestra, on *No Quarter*.

On Record Store Day 2018, an 'Olympic Studios Mix', removing the orchestration of the original version, was issued as a yellow vinyl 7″ single, on the B-side of a 'Sunset Sound Mix' of 'Rock and Roll'.

3. 'Celebration Day' (Jones, Page, Plant) 3.29

A return to high-voltage rock with a smattering of funk, this flows from the previous track as it opens with a frenzied intro of guitar chords played at high speed on top of a monotonic drone from Jones's synthesiser. It came about through an accident. The beginning, Page noted, was inadvertently erased by an assistant engineer:

> ... a terrible mistake.... The bloke just ran out, in case he was going to get killed!... Between 'Friends' and 'Celebration Day', there's this drone that brings the track in, there's part of the vocal, and then it comes into the rhythm, and I put that together as a salvage job after having lost it.[3]

Page therefore used the synth drone from the end of the previous track to fill the gap that had been left. Part of the guitar work was done with a guitar in standard tuning and part on slide guitar, tuned probably to an open 'A'.

When they played it on the 1971 American tour, Plant often called it 'The New York' song as his lyrics were based upon his impressions of the city. The title was adopted many years later as the title for the film and album of the group's reunion concert in 2007 with Jason Bonham on drums, released five years later. Page and The Black Crowes also performed it on *Live at the Greek*.

4. 'Since I've Been Loving You' (Jones, Page, Plant) 7.25

The album's sole excursion into blues territory, it was also the longest track. Borrowing a riff at the start from The Yardbirds' 'New York City Blues', it is a blues in the key of 'C' minor, and it would become a live performance staple for the band as their slow blues showcase, with Page's guitar solo featured both on the recorded version and in the band's live show. One of the first songs to be prepared for the album, it was recorded live in the studio with little overdubbing and was reportedly the hardest to record. Jones plays Hammond organ, using bass pedals for the bassline. When Page came to oversee the compilation of the first CD boxed set in 1990, he realised that Bonham's bass drum pedal was squeaking, and though it went unnoticed at the time, after listening to the master tapes again, it sounded louder every time he heard it. The opening and closing lyrics are similar to 'Now', a track on Moby Grape's 1968 album *Grape Jam*.

It became a regular feature on their set list during most of the American tours, and from 1977 onwards, Page used it to incorporate part of his solo from 'Tea For One'. Live versions are included on *BBC Sessions*, *The Song Remains the Same*, and on *Celebration Day*, the recording of the reformation O2 Arena concert. Other artists, including Europe and Corinne Bailey Rae, have recorded their own versions.

5. 'Out on the Tiles' (Bonham, Page, Plant) 4.05

Being known as a man who enjoyed a drink or two, Bonham was fond of the expression 'out on the tiles'—in other words, visiting the pubs. He used to sing a few lines of doggerel about being 'out on the tiles', of dubious political correctness. Plant was thus inspired to write a more acceptable lyric on the theme, although the words of the title are nowhere to be found in what reads more like a love song than anything else. As the original idea for the song was really his, Bonham was given a joint writing credit. Page worked it up into a guitar riff, with what he called 'close miking and distance miking' to achieve ambient sound, or 'getting the distance of the time lag from one end of the room to the other'. It is arguably one of the less interesting tracks on the album, with almost the last half of the four minutes featuring the same guitar pattern—chords, rather than solo, and Plant's repeated ad-libbed 'ooh yeah' *ad infinitum*, until the fade.

When the deluxe remastered edition was released in June 2014, the second disc included an instrumental version, 'Bathroom Sound Track (No Vocal)', thus named as on the first playback everyone said it sounded as if the drums had been recorded in the bathroom.

It featured only briefly in the live set, during the American tour of summer 1970 shortly before the album's original release, although the intro was later used with performances of 'Black Dog' on stage on *How The West Was Won*, and again later at Knebworth in 1979. The intro was also used with Bonham's drum solo 'Over the Top' on the North American 1977 tour. Page performed it with The Black Crowes on tour in 1999 and on *Live at the Greek*.

6. 'Gallows Pole' (Traditional, arranged Page, Plant) 4.56

This started life as an old traditional folk song, 'The Maid Freed from the Gallows', about a woman using bribery to escape execution. Several variations are known, among them 'The Gallis Pole' as recorded in 1939 by Leadbelly (Huddie Ledbetter), and under the title above in 1970 by Fred Gerlach. Page was inspired partly by the latter's version, partly by one on the B-side of a single from 1965 by Dorris Henderson, an African-American singer who performed regularly at British folk clubs around that time, under the title of 'Hangman'. On the group recording, he plays a banjo that he had borrowed off Jones, although it was the first time he had ever tried anything on the instrument: 'I just picked it up and started moving my fingers around until the chords sounded right, which is the same way I work on compositions when the guitar's in different tunings'.[4] He also uses six-string and twelve-string acoustic, and Gibson Les Paul electric guitar, while Jones adds mandolin as well as bass guitar. From a fairly relaxed tempo at the beginning, it gradually speeds up, especially when Bonham brings the drums in about two minutes after the start.

Mandolins were much in evidence in British rock at this time, partly due to Led Zeppelin's use of them on this album and the next, partly due to the success of McGuinness Flint's 'When I'm Dead and Gone', a No. 2 hit at the end of 1970, and also through their use by Lindisfarne who had just released their first album *Nicely Out of Tune*. One of the group's mandolin players, Ray Jackson, gave the instrument an even higher profile through his work as a session musician on Rod Stewart's solo material in the early 1970s, especially the closing section on 'Maggie May'.

In Led Zeppelin's version of the song, the lyrics and outcome of the tale have been altered. The hangman pockets the money, and still does his grisly work: 'But now I laugh and pull so hard, and see you swinging on the Gallows Pole'.

Their live performances of it were few and far between, confined mainly to dates at Copenhagen and Liverpool in May 1971 and Ipswich that November.

On the 1975 American tour, Plant included a few of the lyrics in 'Trampled Underfoot', when he introduced it as 'Trampled Under Gallows'. During Page and Plant's work together on *Unledded* and their subsequent tours up to 1998, it returned to the set, and again when Plant went on tour with Strange Sensation in 2003 and Band of Joy in 2010.

7. 'Tangerine' (Page) 3.10

This uncharacteristically pretty song about lost love was considered to be rather in the style of early Neil Young or perhaps Donovan, one of the unofficial high priests of British folk music and flower power in the 1960s, and on several of whose sessions Page and Jones had played.

It is one of the two Zeppelin non-instrumentals from their recording career attributed to Page as the sole songwriter; the credit for the other, 'Dazed and Confused', was later altered. Not for the first time in their history, its authorship has been the subject of dispute. The guitarist first recorded it as a member of The Yardbirds at Columbia Studios, New York City, in April 1968, as a demo with the title 'Knowing That I'm Losing You'. The sessions remained unreleased as the group was then close to disbanding. Page's composition of the melody is beyond dispute, though he claimed that the lyrics were all his own work, penned 'after an old emotional upheaval' and altered a little. The previous title does not appear in the very sparse lyrics that comprise this version. Two former Yardbirds maintained that their vocalist and lyricist Keith Relf was responsible, as did his sister, Jane, although they never copyrighted the song.

The second shortest number on the album, it opens with a few seconds of delicately picked guitar, stops, and then allows Page to whisper a count-in before starting again. He plays two guitar parts throughout, one on a six-string and the other on a twelve-string acoustic guitar, which almost sound as one, with pedal steel guitar fills later on, plus a short break on heavily sustained Gibson Les Paul, double-tracked—as is Plant's vocal in places, harmonising with himself. For the second track in a row, Jones adds mandolin as well as bass guitar, while Bonham's drums are restrained, not coming in until one minute on and later pausing for effect. In places, the pastoral mood of this song can be seen as something of a dress rehearsal for the gentler passages of the epic 'Stairway to Heaven' a few months later.

Plant sometimes introduced this on stage as a number for their families and people they had been close to, 'a song of love at its most innocent stages'. It was a regular feature on the set list from the Japanese dates in September 1971 up to the American dates the following summer, and then dropped until the Earl's Court shows in 1975 when they performed it in four-part harmony, with Page playing the Gibson double-neck guitar. Page and Plant featured it on their 1995–96 and 1998 world tours, and Plant revived it on his world tour with Band of Joy in 2010–11.

8. 'That's The Way' (Page, Plant) 5.38

At over five minutes, this is the album's second longest number, and in its addressing of social concerns, it is probably their most thought-provoking lyric yet. Page explained that it was written one day after a long walk coming down a ravine and they were setting back to the cottage. They had a guitar and tape recorder with them, and inspiration struck as they stopped and sat down: Page played the tune and Plant sang the first verse straight off. With an original working title of 'The Boy Next Door', some of the lyrics reflected Plant's views on the ecology and environment, hence references to fish dying in dirty waters. Others dwelt on how they had been treated in America during the initial tours when they were spat on, had guns drawn on them, and were heckled at airports and on planes because of their long hair, and on their concerns about the violence they had seen policemen use against protesters against the war in Vietnam, and on fans at their shows.

On the studio recording, Page plays acoustic guitar in open 'G' flat tuning, pedal steel, dulcimer, and bass guitar, with Jones on mandolin and Bonham coming in on tambourine towards the end.

It was one of the songs that gained them respect, even praise, in an unlikely quarter. Journalist Lester Bangs of *Rolling Stone*, who had previously attacked the group for 'insensitive grossness', wrote in his review that this was the first he had heard from them which really moved him, calling it 'beautiful'.

Premiered on stage at the 1970 Bath Festival, it was a regular feature of their acoustic set up to and including the 1972 American tour, and brought back for the Earl's Court shows three years later, with live versions recorded on *BBC Sessions*, *How the West Was Won*, and the *Led Zeppelin* DVD. Page and Plant featured it on their *Unledded* show in 1994 and subsequent world tour, as did Jones on his 2001 tour. It also became one of the few songs in their catalogue that they allowed to be used on a movie soundtrack, for Cameron Crowe's comedy drama *Almost Famous* in 2000.

9. 'Bron-Y-Aur Stomp' (Jones, Page, Plant) 4.17

This cheery four minutes of jug band skiffle, very much in the tradition of Lonnie Donegan on the one hand or Mungo Jerry, the major British music success story of summer 1970, on the other. Named after the cottage where Page and Plant stayed, it means 'golden breast' or hillside of gold in Welsh. The title was misspelt on the album sleeve and label, and when they realised, some four years later, their instrumental 'Bron-Yr-Aur Stomp' on *Physical*

Graffiti would show the correct spelling. In the lyrics, Plant sings a carefree celebration of walking down leafy country lanes with a dog for company, accompanied by Page's Martin D-28 acoustic guitar, Jones's stand-up double bass, and Bonham's spoons and castanets.

Some years later, it was reported that the gentleman who purchased the property in 1972, having been told at the time that 'some pop musicians' had once stayed there, was asking Led Zeppelin fans to respect his privacy and stop coming to visit the premises.

Like several other songs on the album as mentioned above, it was often featured in the group's live acoustic set, from the British tour of winter 1971 to the 1973 European dates. Jones played upright bass and Bonham sang harmony vocals with Plant, stopping in the middle of the third verse. On the 1977 American tour, it was played as a medley with 'Black Country Woman'.

10. 'Hats Off to (Roy) Harper' (Traditional, arranged Charles Obscure) 3.42

Charles Obscure was a pseudonym for Page, who based this on Bukka White's 1937 song 'Shake 'Em On Down'.

Sonically, the track is something of a curiosity. Page plays bottleneck acoustic guitar, while Plant sings through a vibrato amp, giving a slightly distorted effect, rather like hearing an old vintage blues record remastered from a 78 rpm disc—were it not for the fact that the guitar comes mainly from one stereo channel and the voice from the other. Jones and Bonham are not heard on this track. Some detractors have dismissed it as an unintelligible mess, a half-baked concoction of guitar chords and annoying vocals in sore need of being polished. It was one of several traditional blues numbers the duo recorded at the sessions, but the only one they used until the remasters appeared in 2014.

The words have, at best, a tenuous connection with Harper, the contemporary folk singer whom the group had befriended while he was sharing the bill with them at the Bath Festival earlier that year. Page played guitar on his next album, and the group invited him to open for them on some of their subsequent tours. When he was visiting the group's office in Oxford Street one day, Page gave him a copy of the album and told him to look at it. Harper twirled the rotating wheel on the front of the sleeve and told him it was 'very nice and all that'. Only on being urged to look more closely was he touched and flattered to see his name in the title of the last track.

As for why the group named the track thus—for Harper to have his name featured so prominently, in a track listing on the sleeve of a No. 1 album, was the kind of advertising that money could not buy. Page said that, as far as he was concerned, 'hats off to anybody who does what they think is right and refuses to sell out'.[5]

An alternative studio outtake in the same style and similar instrumentation appeared on some bootlegs, and it is assumed to be from the same recording session as the take on the album. It includes lyrics adapted from songs including Robert Johnson's '32-20 Blues' and 'Traveling Riverside Blues', Bukka White's 'Fixin' to Die', Arthur Crudup's 'That's All Right Mama', and Sleepy John Estes's 'Diving Duck Blues'. These were among the songs sometimes performed in medleys on stage by the group during 'How Many More Times' and 'Whole Lotta Love', thus suggesting why they were inspired to record an acoustic studio version of something that had so far been combined to their live performances. In spite of this, they never played it live.

Bonus Tracks

'Bathroom Sound' (Bonham, Page, Plant) 4.00

A rough instrumental mix of 'Out on the Tiles', which fades out a few seconds earlier but otherwise does not essentially differ from the backing on the finished product.

'Jennings Farm Blues' (Jones, Page, Plant) 5.54

An electric version of 'Bron-Y-Aur Stomp', almost six minutes long, with a bustling, bluesy feel closer in spirit to the adrenalin rush of 'Immigrant Song'. The title refers to Plant's farm property at the time in Blakeshall. There was speculation at one time that a finished version of this, or else the relatively commercial 'Baby Come On Home' (see p. 115), would be the track that they were briefly considering for release as a single in early 1970.

'Key to the Highway/Trouble in Mind' (Big Bill Broonzy, Charlie Segar, Richard M. Jones) 4.05

This medley of two blues standards sounds more like an informal jam session than a track intended for release. The first number was originally recorded by Charlie Segar in 1940 and many other artists since then—most famously of all in 1970 by Eric Clapton with Derek and the Dominos—while the second, written by Richard M. Jones in 1924, and again much covered over the years, features only Page and Plant, who plays harmonica as well as sings, presumably through a vibrato amp and thus achieving the same distorted, ersatz vintage effect as on 'Hats Off to (Roy) Harper'.

4

[*Led Zeppelin IV—untitled album*]

UK: released 12 November 1971, Atlantic, No. 1 for two weeks (2014 reissue, No. 6)
US: released 8 November 1971, Atlantic, No. 2
Current edition: Atlantic CD
Personnel: Robert Plant—lead and backing vocals, harmonica, tambourine
Jimmy Page—electric and acoustic guitars, mandolin
John Paul Jones—bass guitar, acoustic guitar, electric piano, mandolin, recorders, EMS VCS 3 synthesizer
John Bonham—drums, percussion
Sandy Denny—vocals (track 3)
Ian Stewart—piano (track 2)
Recorded at Rolling Stones Mobile Studio, Headley Grange, Hampshire; Island Studios, London; Olympic Studios, London, November 1970–January 1971
Produced by Jimmy Page

Shortly after the release of *III*, Page told the press that he was already planning the next album, which would be more versatile and use more combinations of different instruments. One side would contain one long track featuring 'mandolin, banjo and so on', lasting about twenty-five minutes. This was not fully realised, but the record did indeed feature one ambitious number that came close to eclipsing their previous recorded achievements and would leave them with one that proved difficult to surpass.

The whole album was recorded over a three-month period, mostly at Headley Grange and London, mixed in Los Angeles and again in London after the initial American mix proved unsatisfactory. Eleven tracks emerged from the sessions, three being held over and appearing on the subsequent double album *Physical Graffiti*.

Chastened by a mixed critical reception and to some extent disappointing sales for the third album, Page decided that their fourth would be totally anonymous in having no title, and that their name, the track titles, and even the catalogue number would not appear on the sleeve. Instead, the inner bag featured symbols representing each member, and it has since been variously referred to as '*Zoso*' (the visual equivalent of Page's symbol), '*Four Symbols*', '*The Fourth Led Zeppelin Album*', and '*Untitled*'.

Page's symbol, which looks like the word 'Zoso', was designed by himself to represent a sigil, connected with magician Aleister Crowley, although he has declined to explain fully its meaning or significance. Jones's is a single circle intersecting a triquetra or trefoil, chosen from calligrapher Rudolf Koch's *Book of Signs*, as was Bonham's three interlocking rings, while Plant designed his own—of a feather within a circle. When the group toured Britain in the winter of 1971, shortly after the album's release, they visually projected the four symbols on their stage equipment.

Page was warned by Atlantic that his tactics of launching an outwardly anonymous album would be 'commercial suicide', but he insisted that names and titles meant nothing, and meant to let the music speak for itself (a logical conclusion to this might have been to deny each track its own title and even have blank labels on the record inside). His tactics were vindicated, as the record was an immediate massive global commercial and critical success, and has regularly been cited in all-time best albums lists over the years. Some regard it as the artistic peak of their whole career.

The photograph on the front of the sleeve shows a nineteenth-century oil painting of an elderly man gathering sticks, bought by Plant at a Reading antique shop, hanging on the papered wall of a partly demolished suburban house. The block of flats on the back of the sleeve is Salisbury Tower, Ladywood, Birmingham. Page's explanation was that the design was intended to convey a message, using images of the old countryman and the blocks of flats being knocked down to say that mankind should look after the earth instead of destroying everything. The inside of the gatefold design, 'The Hermit', shows a favourite Tarot card image of Page. According to rumour, the artist was Barrington Colby, a reclusive friend of Page's who lived in Switzerland—or perhaps even a pseudonym of the former art school student turned guitarist himself.

A remastered reissue in October 2014 comprised six formats: a standard CD edition, a deluxe two-CD edition, a standard LP version, a deluxe two-LP version, a super deluxe two-CD plus two-LP version with a hardback book, and as high-resolution 96k/24-bit digital downloads. The deluxe and super deluxe editions feature alternate mixes of each track.

Tracks

1. 'Black Dog' (Jones, Page, Plant) 4.55

Jones was inspired to help create a track based on 'electric blues with a rolling bass part' after listening to Muddy Waters's 1968 album *Electric Mud*, and he wrote the riff on the back of a train ticket one day while travelling between his home and Page's houseboat for rehearsals. He intended it to be built on complex rhythm changes that people could not dance to, and that despite the apparently simple drum pattern, the complex shifting time signature was a deliberate attempt to make it difficult for other acts to copy, although in a subsequent interview, he claimed this was a fabrication. However, he wanted the song recorded in 6/8 time, but they realised it would be too hard to reproduce live, so Bonham eliminated the 5/4 variation, allowing Plant to perform the *a cappella* vocal interludes and for the instruments to come back in together. A careful listen will reveal Bonham tapping his drumsticks together before each riff, in order to keep time and to send a signal to the rest of them. It has been suggested that the stop-start routine was also partly inspired by Fleetwood Mac's 'Oh Well', or perhaps even Mose Allison's 'Young Man Blues', as recently and memorably covered by The Who on their album *Live at Leeds*.

Page built up his solo from four overdubbed fills on his Gibson Les Paul, with the sounds at the beginning being those of the guitar warming up or, in his words, 'waking up the army of guitars'. Plant recorded his vocals in two takes, and in live performances, his 'ah-ah' refrains became a call-and-response routine between him and the audience.

The subject matter is nothing to do with animals, or even about depression, and not for the first time in their catalogue, the title does not appear in the song. Plant admitted it was one of his 'blatant-let's-do-it-in-the-bath-type thing' lyrics that was not 'meant to be scrutinised', thus giving the lie to theories that the black dog was a hellhound with some kind of Satanic connection. In fact, the animal was a nameless black Labrador Retriever that wandered the grounds at Headley Grange, and when the group did not have an obvious name for the track, this was the first thing that occurred to them.

In several territories throughout the world, it was the first single from the album, with 'Misty Mountain Hop' on the B-side, reaching No. 15 in America.

It was a regular feature in live performances since being premiered at Ulster Hall, Belfast, in March 1971, several months before its initial release on record, and in concert over the next couple of years, sometimes with the first few bars of 'Out on the Tiles' as the introduction. In 1975, it was featured as an encore medley with 'Whole Lotta Love', and returned to the set for Knebworth in 1979 and the final European tour the following summer. Page and Plant played it on their world tours between 1995 and 1998, and Page retained it in the set while touring Japan with David Coverdale in 2003. Jones performed an instrumental version on his 1999 and 2001 tours, and Plant also featured it while touring with Band of Joy in 2010. Five years later, it was used as a commercial for a video game, *Destiny: The Taken King*, with game action taking place as the song could be heard in the background.

Among those who have recorded cover versions are CCS, Eumir Deodato, Deborah Harry, John Farnham, Heart (on two different live albums), and the appropriately named, but unrelated Tracy Bonham. In 2010, Slash named it as his favourite guitar riff of all time.

2. 'Rock and Roll' (Bonham, Jones, Page, Plant) 3.40

Had the group been more singles-minded, this track would have surely been on its knees crying out for 45 rpm release in Britain. Sometimes three chords are all you need, and three chords were all it took on what in Page's words was 'a spontaneous combustion'. They were trying without success to complete the recording of 'Four Sticks', but 'it just wasn't happening' so they put it on one side and decided to loosen up with a jam session instead. Bonham played the beginning of 'Keep A-Knockin'', Page added a guitar riff based on the same song and other rock 'n' roll classics, Plant ad-libbed lyrics with references to oldies such as 'The Stroll', 'The Book of Love', and 'Walking in the Moonlight'', and Ian Stewart, 'the sixth Rolling Stone', joined in on piano. For Page, once he had started playing the riff, 'it was just so exciting that we thought, "let's just work on this". The riff and the sequence was really immediate to those 12-bar patterns that you had in those old rock songs like Little Richard, etc., and it was just so spur-of-the-moment the way that it just came together more or less out of nowhere.'[1] On another occasion, he recalled that it 'ground to a halt after about twelve bars, but it was enough to know that there was enough of a number there to keep working on it. Robert even came in singing on it straight away'.[2]

It was chosen as the second single off the album in several countries, usually with 'Four Sticks' or, in the case of South Africa, 'Going to California' on the B-side. In America, it reached No. 47.

For three years, the group made it the opening number of all concert performances, after which it became part of a medley encore with 'Whole Lotta Love', and on the 1979 and 1980 shows, it was a standalone encore. The surviving members then used it to open their three-song Live Aid set in July 1985. Plant initially used to refer to it on stage by the first line, 'It's Been a Long Time'. In June 2008, Page and Jones joined the Foo Fighters for a performance of it on stage at Wembley Stadium, with Dave Grohl on drums (instead of his usual guitar) and usual drummer Taylor Hawkins on vocal. Plant performed it while touring with Alison Krauss that same year.

Over the years, several others have recorded their own versions, among them Vanilla Fudge, Stevie Nicks, Van Halen, Sheryl Crow, John Waite, Steve Lukather, Great White, Chris Norman, Jerry Lee Lewis (with Page on guitar), and, most bizarrely of all, Alvin and the Chipmunks. The song also featured on a charity single, credited to tennis stars John McEnroe, Pat Cash and the Full Metal Rackets, with Roger Daltrey on lead vocal and two members of Iron Maiden, bassist Steve Harris and drummer Nicko McBrain, in the one-off group, with proceeds going to Rock Aid Armenia. It made the chart for one week in July 1991 at No. 66.

In 2001, the original recording became the first Led Zeppelin song ever licensed for a television series, when it was used in an episode of the American comedy drama *The Sopranos*. One year later, it was licensed for use in a series of television adverts from General Motors, and in 2011, it was featured as the opening theme of a Serbian documentary series, *Rockovnik*, tracing the history of Yugoslav rock music.

On Record Store Day 2018, a 'Sunset Sound Mix' was issued as a yellow vinyl 7″ single, backed by the 'Olympic Studios Mix' of 'Friends', removing the orchestration of the original version.

3. 'The Battle of Evermore' (Page, Plant) 5.52

A reversion to the predominantly acoustic stylings of the previous album, this was the only song the group ever recorded on which they featured a guest vocalist. Page wrote the music at Headley Grange while experimenting on a mandolin, a happy accident of sorts. The instrument belonged to Jones, and at a particular moment when nothing was happening, he picked it up, started improvising a chord sequence out of the blue, and it all came together at once. 'Listening to it now,' he said some ten years later, 'it seems strange that it was really the first time I'd ever played a mandolin … probably pretty basic chords, but the end result was really great.'[3] When they recorded it, he only played mandolin, with Jones on acoustic guitar instead of bass.

Plant's inspiration for the lyrics was the combination of a book on Scottish history he had recently been reading, and his fascination with Tolkien's *Lord of the Rings*. The theme is fantasy, in part a description of the battle of the Pelennor Fields from *The Return of the King*, with its references to characters such as Aragorn ('The prince of peace'), Éowyn ('The queen of light'), Sauron ('The dark lord'), and the Ringwraiths (who 'ride in black'). Diluting the exclusively Middle-Earth aura, and instead focusing on one particular legend is a mention for the 'angels of Avalon', a distinct reference to Arthurian lore.[4]

When they had written it, he felt the piece was not so much a song as a playlet, and they needed another voice to combine with his in telling the story. He had been a friend of Sandy Denny, former member of Fairport Convention, since they shared the same bill at Bath in the summer of 1970, and he invited her to duet with him as the lyrics required him to play the role of the narrator and someone else the town crier, who would urge the people to throw down their weapons. They alternate on some of the lines and harmonise on others. To thank Denny for her involvement in providing her angelic, almost other-worldly contributions, she was given her own symbol on the album sleeve, and chose one showing three pyramids. It had been hard work for her, as the session left her quite hoarse: '... having someone out-sing you is a horrible feeling'.[5]

In retrospect, some twenty years later, Plant admitted that it suffered a little from naïveté and tweeness—he was only twenty-three at the time—but 'it makes up for it in the cohesion of the voices and the playing'.[6]

The group played it in concert on the 1977 North American tour, with Jones singing Denny's vocals and playing acoustic guitar while Page reprised his work on mandolin, and Bonham occasionally sang along with Jones, as well as playing tambourine with a mallet. Page and Plant recorded another version in 1994 on the *No Quarter* album, with Najma Akhtar reprising Denny's role. Plant also performed it while touring with Alison Krauss in 2008, and in August that year, he made a guest appearance with Fairport Convention at the Cropredy Festival, duetting with Kristina Donahue, daughter of ex-Fairport guitarist Jerry Donahue.

4. 'Stairway to Heaven' (Page, Plant) 8.02

For ten years, the title 'Stairway to Heaven' was associated with an American Top 10 hit of 1960 by Neil Sedaka, and some years before that with the B-side of a Slim Whitman single. Then Led Zeppelin claimed it as their own, using it for an ambitious eight-minute epic of sections each gradually increasing in volume and tempo, or to quote Page, speeding up 'like an adrenaline flow'.

It began early in 1970 when Page worked on initial ideas for a major new number to replace 'Dazed and Confused' as the focal point of their stage show, trying out sections on guitar in the eight-track studio in his boathouse. That spring, he had decided he wanted a really epic song on the next album, or the next after that, and told the music press that they did not want to say too much about it in case the idea did not work—but they intended to try something new with the organ and acoustic guitar 'building up and building to the electric thing'. It continued to take shape after being worked on at Bron-Yr-Aur, and after several months' gestation, recording began at the end of the year.

As he was running through pieces on acoustic and electric guitars, Plant was busy writing, then got up and started singing. His initial lyrics were mainly spontaneously improvised and, Page claimed, many were written there and then. Plant later said that he was writing out the words: 'There's a lady is sure [sic.], all that glitters is gold, and she's buying a stairway to heaven'. He sat there, looked at them, and almost leapt out of his seat. His explanation of the lyrics was that they were about a woman getting everything she wanted all the time without giving anything back, someone who accumulates money, only to find out the hard way her life has no meaning and it will not get her into heaven. His aim, he said, was to try and bring 'the remote, pastoral Britain, the old, almost unspoken Celtic references into the piece'.

Always an admirer of all things mystic, old English legends and lore in general, and *The Lord of the Rings* by J. R. R. Tolkien and *Magic Arts in Celtic Britain* by the British antiquarian Lewis Spence, he cited these as a source for his lyrics. The Tolkien inspiration comes in the phrase, 'In my thoughts I have seen rings of smoke through the trees,' apparently a reference to smoke rings blown by the wizard Gandalf. There is also a correlation between the woman in the song and Tolkien's Lady Galadriel, the Queen of Elves, who lived in the forest of Lothlórien. In the book, all that glittered around her was gold, as the leaves of the trees in the forest were golden.

'In the rehearsal, Robert was very quiet while he wrote most of the lyrics, then he just let fire!' Page later recalled.[7] He felt Plant's lyrics were his finest yet, and they became the first by the group ever printed on an inner album sleeve, 'so that people could really concentrate on it'.[8] For him, the song crystallised the essence of the band:

> It had everything there and showed the band at its best.... It was a milestone for us. Every musician wants to do something of lasting quality, something which will hold up for a long time and I guess we did it with 'Stairway' ... I don't know whether I have the ability to come up with more. I have to do a lot of hard work before I can get anywhere near those stages of consistent, total brilliance.[9]

The song begins slowly and gracefully with Page's acoustic guitar and Jones's overlaid recorders playing in Renaissance style, moving after two minutes into a slow electric section. Just over four minutes in, the piano, drums, and electric instruments enter. At this point, Bonham took a while to get the timing right when they began recording. Five and a half minutes in follows a hard rock segment based on three descending chords, 'Am', 'G', and 'F' (calling to mind Dylan's 'All Along the Watchtower'), dominated by Plant's impassioned vocal in a higher range and Page's solo speeding up to a crescendo and then the final, unaccompanied 'And she's buying a stairway to heaven'. Page had devised another guitar part with which to finish it, but decided not to use it since the *a cappella* vocal created the right impact. He used electric six- and twelve-string guitars and an acoustic six-string on the recording, and when playing it on stage, he used a double-neck guitar comprising six and twelve strings while Jones initially used a Mellotron and later a Yamaha Grand Piano and GHX-1 synthesiser, or a Hohner electric piano.

The song breaks one of the time-honoured musical rules—or does it? Talking about it thirty years later, Page looked back on his and Jones's early days as session musicians:

> [The] cardinal sin [was] to speed up. And I thought, right, we'll do something that speeds up. But that, seriously, was another thing we always did in Zeppelin. If it started to move in tempo, don't worry, it's finding its own tempo. Don't worry, just all stay together.[10]

It received its first broadcast on 4 April on Radio 1 as part of a live concert recorded three days earlier by the BBC at the Paris Cinema, London. The group had already given it its live debut on what was their first appearance in Northern Ireland, at Ulster Hall, Belfast, on 5 March 1971. The audience seemed unimpressed, and Jones thought they were 'all bored to tears waiting to hear something they knew'. Only after a subsequent performance on the American tour in August—where about a third of them gave the group a standing ovation—did they realised that they had something really special. Page always vividly remembered the standing ovation they received:

> And I thought: 'This is incredible, because no one's heard this number yet. This is the first time they're hearing it!' It obviously touched them, you know. And that was at the L.A. Forum, so I knew we were onto something with that one.[11]

It soon had a regular place as the grand finale of their show, sometimes lasting ten minutes or more, with Page playing an extended solo and Plant adding light-hearted ad-libs such as 'Does anybody remember laughter?', 'Does anybody remember forests?', or 'And I think you can see that'. At length, he became disenchanted with having it constantly on the set list, saying that there were only so many times he could sing it and really mean it, and it was becoming sanctimonious. During the 1980s, he had to be persuaded to do so on special occasions, such as at Live Aid in July 1985 (where he was astonished to see Duran Duran crying at the side of the stage while they were on), or at the Atlantic Records fortieth anniversary show at Madison Square Garden in May 1988. Later that year, he said that he would 'break out in hives' if he had to sing it in every show. He had written the lyrics 'and found that song to be of some importance and consequence in 1971, but 17 years later, I don't know. It's just not for me. I sang it at the Atlantic Records show because I'm an old softie and it was my way of saying thank you to Atlantic because

I've been with them for 20 years. But no more of "Stairway to Heaven" for me.'[12] Within a few years, he had come to terms with the millstone around his neck, but a sense of ambivalence remained. At a press conference in 2012, he admitted that he struggled with some of the lyrics from particular periods of time: 'Maybe I was still trying to work out what I was talking about'.[13]

Allegations that chords for the song had been lifted from 'And She's Lonely', a track by the Chocolate Watch Band with whom The New Yardbirds had shared billing with in 1968, never went any further. Yet another case did not fade away quite as quietly. The song became the subject of legal action after similarities were pointed out between the introduction and 'Taurus', a guitar instrumental written by Randy California of Spirit and recorded by them in 1968. That year, they had toured with Led Zeppelin, who played the Spirit tune 'Fresh Garbage' in their set, and Page admitted he owned a copy of the album. California, real name Randy Wolfe, died in 1997. Not long before his death, he told the press that he had been 'ripped off.... And the guys made millions of bucks on it and never said "Thank you," never said, "Can we pay you some money for it?" It's a kind of sore point with me.'

In 2014, one of his trustees and another member of Spirit filed a copyright infringement suit against the group, in an effort to secure a co-writing credit for the late guitarist and a share of future profits for his estate and the publishers. When it came to court in Los Angeles in June 2016, the group's attorney, Peter Anderson, said the case was an attempt to rewrite history, 'to take an iconic song ... and say it's got a new parent'.[14] Page, Plant, and their counsel maintained that the descending minor chord progression was a common building block of classical and popular music, dating back three centuries, and could be found in popular music predating 'Taurus'. Their claim was backed by Lawrence Ferrara, a Music Professor at New York University. He maintained that the likeness of one composition to the other was limited, and that comparing differences in the arrangement of the same notes in both songs was like rearranging the letters in 'treason' to spell 'senator', noting that the succession of letters makes a difference: '... it's not something anyone can own'.[15] The jury ruled in favour of the group and dismissed the case on the grounds that similarities between the songs did not amount to copyright infringement, as the chord progression was common to many other songs and therefore in the public domain.

Throughout the years, group and management resisted all efforts by Atlantic to release it as a single, apart from strictly limited promotional and jukebox pressings. It therefore became one of the most heavily played album tracks of all time despite its eight-minute length and, unlike 'Whole Lotta Love', being almost impossible for radio programmers to edit or fade. Page insisted that they wanted people to hear it in the context of the album, and it would help the album sell if it was not available separately. There was another reason:

'... one thing I would never have entertained was messing around with that song. I knew that the minute it was a single, the next thing they would want it to be an edited version, and I wasn't having that, no way'.[16] In Australia, it appeared on a three-track EP *Acoustically*, with 'Going to California' and 'The Battle of Evermore' in 1972.

Almost twenty years on, in 1990, promotional 7" copies were issued in Britain—a strictly limited edition of 150 copies in 1990 for radio stations—at the same time as the compilation CD *Remasters*, number LZ3, and for jukeboxes, with a slightly different catalogue number (LZ3 LC), with 'Whole Lotta Love' on the B-side. In America, a 12" single surfaced, thought to be a poor quality sound bootleg. An American 7" picture disc, again probably a bootleg, was released in 1980 with 'Hey, Hey, What Can I Do' on the B-side.

Technical considerations prevailed in the world of early 1970s vinyl technology. As an eight-minute track, it would have fitted on to a 45 rpm 7" single, but none too happily. Because of its length, the disc would have required very shallow grooves compared to one for a song with half the playing time or less, a much narrower stereo field, and lower volume, thus vulnerable to surface noise from scratches and stylus wear. If played regularly, the sound quality would rapidly deteriorate, particularly in the quieter passages (this did not prevent the release in 1971 of Steppenwolf's 'For Madmen Only', on a B-side, and in 1976 of Lynyrd Skynyrd's 'Free Bird', both around a minute longer than 'Stairway', and both at 45 rpm, though the former is very quiet, even ambient all the way through, and the latter relatively low volume until the fast section takes over after about five minutes). The alternative would be a maxi-single with a speed of 33 rpm, which would likewise have impacted on audio quality and volume.

In the 1980s, television journalists in America claimed that 'Stairway to Heaven' was one of several popular songs that featured backmasking, or hidden messages. If played backwards, they declared, it sounded as if Plant was singing 'Here's to my sweet Satan' or 'I sing because I live with Satan'. Spokesmen for the group dismissed such allegations as nonsense, saying that their turntables only played in one direction—forwards. It did not stop one fan from posting what he claimed were the full backwards lyrics of the song online, beginning with 'Oh ask me of the wars of Beelzebub', and including such little gems as 'Did you hear me Lord? I first give to Satan' and 'There was cat burglar, bit off my leg'.

As with any overwhelmingly popular song heavily played, written about, argued over, and dissected over the years, it has attracted its fair share of non-fans and those who claim it is overrated, or that they never wish to hear it again. Familiarity breeds contempt, and some guitar shops apparently ban customers from playing the intro on their premises or threaten to fine them if they must. As far as we know, nobody has yet made headlines by being taken for court for refusing to pay up. At the same time, it is equally revered for its startling, if not unique qualities. Ann Wilson of Heart, a group who often covered the group's songs on concert to the extent that they were sometimes dubbed 'Little Led Zeppelin', has called it 'a complete marriage of music to lyrics.... We all know it's inspired by Tolkien, but at the same time they're widened out so they're more universal than that. Those were such optimistic words that fit with the whole hippie mentality. I think people really identified with the lyrics.'[17]

It was highly placed on many journalists' and listeners' polls. John Peel's first-ever Festive Fifty on Radio 1 in December 1976, for which listeners voted just as punk rock was starting to take over the show, placed it at No. 1, while his colleague, Alan Freeman, once joked that the ideal way for him to meet his maker would be to have a heart attack after having just put the record on the turntable.[18] A survey of 'the best album of all time' in *The Times* in 1993 placed the whole record at No. 18, and labelled 'Stairway' as 'pomp rock's most enduring anthem', dismissing Plant's lyrics as 'complete tosh', but acknowledging that 'there is real drama as the tension builds, climaxes and dissipates through eight minutes'.[19] Numerous cover versions have been issued, some faithfully attempting to capture the spirit of the original, others wilfully eccentric. Two made the British Top 10, one by Far Corporation in 1985 (No. 8) and another by Rolf Harris in 1993 (No. 7). Other recordings have come from Dolly Parton, Heart, Foo Fighters, U2, Dave Matthews Band, Stanley Jordan, Elkie Brooks, Justin Hayward, Pat Boone, Frank Zappa, and Great White (The O'Jays also recorded a different song with the same title in 1975). In 1978, Little Roger and the Goosebumps released a parody, 'Stairway to Gilligan', based on the American TV sitcom *Gilligan's Island*, but as they had not obtained clearance, Grant took out an injunction that resulted in its withdrawal.

Even the original version eventually reached the British chart—after thirty-six years. From 2005 onwards, as physical singles were becoming a thing of the past, download sales of individual tracks became eligible for the Top 100. In November 2007, Zeppelin mania following their concert at the O2 Arena created such demand for their material that 'Stairway to Heaven' entered the chart for eight weeks, at what would be its highest position, No. 37. Two others charted less strongly at the same time, 'Whole Lotta Love' (No. 64) and 'Kashmir' (No. 80).

5. 'Misty Mountain Hop' (Jones, Page, Plant) 4.38

Some have suggested that the Misty Mountains of the title are those referred to in Tolkien's *The Hobbit*, others that they refer to a mountainous range in Wales, which may have inspired Tolkien. Basically, the song is about events at a 'Legalise pot rally' at Hyde Park, London, on 7 July 1968, in which the police made several arrests for marijuana possession. Plant's lyrics include references to his vision of a more free society, of crowds of people sitting on the grass with flowers in their hair, and of a policeman asking everyone to get in line. In the last verse, the narrator decided he is going to pack his bags for the Misty Mountains, 'over the hills where the spirits fly'.

It was one of the group's quickest and most painless songs to complete. Jones was up early before everybody else one morning and playing around on the electric piano when he hit on the central riff. When the others got up and he gave them an airing, they were already part of the way there.

In America, it was also released on the B-side of 'Black Dog'.

It was featured on the 1971 European tour, on the dates in Japan in 1972 and in America in 1973, after which it was dropped until the Copenhagen and Knebworth 1979 shows. Plant played it on his solo tours, as well as with Page on the 1988 reunion, on a guest spot at Hammersmith that same year, at the Knebworth Silver Clef show in 1990, and on their 1998 world tour. Page retained it in his set with The Black Crowes while touring in 2000, and it reappeared in the O2 Arena show in 2007.

6. 'Four Sticks' (Page, Plant) 4.45

Page said this track was always meant to be 'abstract'. He and Plant wrote it together during a visit to India. It has a slightly hypnotic quality, more akin to an oriental chant than a conventional western rock song. Having tried it several times and simply not getting the feel they wanted, in the early hours one morning, they attempted it again after Bonham had downed a Double Diamond, picked up two sets of four drum sticks, and did it in one take. Page recalled that 'Bonzo' had just been to see Ginger Baker's Airforce 'and he was really hyped about it'. Much as he admired Baker, he was in an 'I'll show him!' frame of mind. He came in, picked up the four sticks, and they completed it in two takes: '... he just took it into another stratosphere'.[20] Much of it is built round Page's guitar riff, with Jones producing a drone-like sound on VCS-3 synthesiser as well as playing bass guitar. Plant's lyrics are ad-libbed and say little, if anything.

The group only played it live once, at K. B. Hallen, Copenhagen, on 3 May 1971 during the summer European tour. Page and Plant revived it on the *Unledded* project in 1994 and on their tour of 1995–96, with Plant retaining it on his tours with Strange Sensation from 2002 to 2006.

7. 'Going to California' (Page, Plant) 3.31

A return to acoustic folk music, this song features Page playing acoustic guitar with a D-A-D-G-B-D tuning, Jones on mandolin, and no bass or drums. Joni

Above: Led Zeppelin, promotional picture, 1968. *Left to right*: John Bonham, Robert Plant, Jimmy Page, and John Paul Jones.

Below: Led Zeppelin's acoustic spot on stage, with Jones on mandolin.

Led Zeppelin, the back cover of the initial album pressing. Note the deliberately misleading timing of the final track.

'Good Times Bad Times/Communication Breakdown', a promotional copy of the debut American single released in March 1969, reaching No. 80.

'Good Times Bad Times/Communication Breakdown', the German release, which failed to chart there, although the debut album reached No. 11 in Germany.

Above: 'Whole Lotta Love/Livin' Lovin' Maid (She's a Woman)', the British single released in December 1969 without the group or management's consent and speedily withdrawn.

Below: CCS, fronted by Alexis Korner (front, second from right), whose version of 'Whole Lotta Love' charted at No. 13 in Britain and was used as the theme music for BBC TV's *Top of the Pops* for several years.

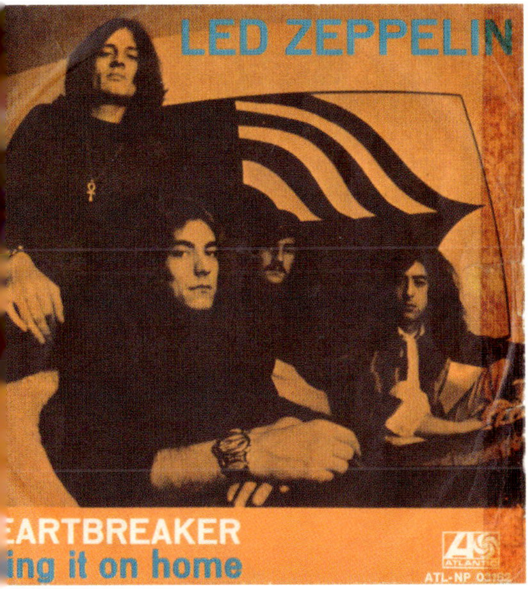

'Heartbreaker/Bring it on Home', the Italian release, with an advertisement for the *musicanastri* (musicassette) of the second album on the reverse

Above left: Bonham, Plant, and Page with Sandy Denny, vocalist with Fairport Convention, at the time of the *Melody Maker* awards, September 1970. Denny, the only singer ever to appear as a guest on a Led Zeppelin record, sang on 'The Battle of Evermore' on the fourth album.

Above right: 'Immigrant Song/Hey, Hey, What Can I Do', the Japanese single release sleeve insert.

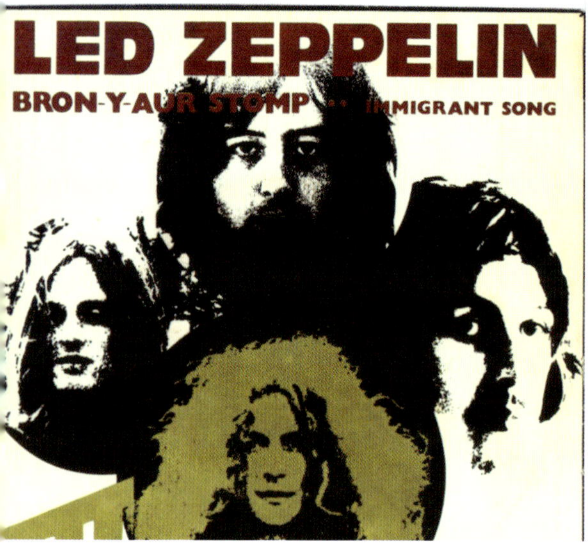

'Bron-Y-Aur Stomp/Immigrant Song', the Italian release.

Led Zeppelin on stage, with the Zoso logo clearly visible on the right.

Led Zeppelin, apparently all whistling at the camera, *c*. 1972.

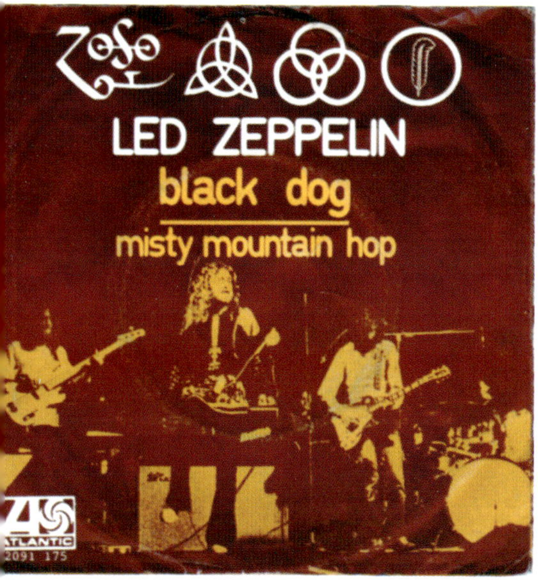

‘Black Dog/Misty Mountain Hop’, the Netherlands release, where it reached No. 20.

‘Misty Mountain Hop/Black Dog’, the Italian release, with the sleeve incorporating *The Hermit*, by Barrington Colby, from the inner gatefold design of the fourth album.

Above left: 'Stairway to Heaven', the American sheet music.

Above right and below: 'Stairway to Heaven', the American twentieth anniversary promotional edition, 1991, with the same track on both sides, and sleeve design based on the outer sleeve of the fourth album.

'Stairway to Heaven/Whole Lotta Love', the British jukebox issue, 1990.

'Stairway to Heaven/Whole Lotta Love', the British promotional issue, 1991.

eastwest records

29th November 1990

electric lighting station
46 kensington court
london w8 5dp
telephone 01 938 2181
telex 261425
facsimile 01 937 6645

Dear All,

Re: LED ZEPPELIN - "Stairway To Heaven"

Although a lot of pressure was put on the band to release this commercially, unfortunately as they have already resisted releasing a single for 10 years, they still won't budge.

In anticipation of them consenting to the release, we pressed 150 promotional copies up-front.

I would imagine that in the future these could quite possibly be a bit of a "collectors item", so I am still servicing them to you to help you all with your pension plans!!!!!

See you at the 1999 Record Fair!

Best,

Sal x

SALLI GRIFFIN

eastwest records is a division of wea records limited registered at above address no 680511 a warner communications company trademark of warner

'Stairway to Heaven', a letter from the press office, EastWest Records, a division of WEA (Warner Elektra Atlantic), London, accompanying the 1990 promotional copy. The group still said no to a full release.

'D'yer Maker/Over the Hills and Far Away', the British promotional copy.

Jimmy Page on stage.

Robert Plant on stage.

John Bonham on stage.

John Paul Jones on stage.

'Trampled Under Foot/Black Country Woman', one of a limited edition of 5,000 singles supplied to British record shops at the time of the 1975 Earls Court concerts. Notice the two-word title on the die-cut sleeve, and absence of catalogue number DC 1 from the label, only visible on the run-out groove.

Led Zeppelin, *c*. 1975.

Right: Jimmy Page with violin bow in hand.

Below: Robert Plant and Jimmy Page share an onstage vocal.

Above: Led Zeppelin on stage.

Below: 'All My Love', a promotional copy of the Brazilian single, mono and stereo, which despite the '4.00' on the label timing is the full five-minute and fifty-three-second album version. It was apparently issued as a single only in certain South American countries.

Mitchell is named as a major influence on Plant's inspiration, undoubtedly because it shares something of the uncomplicated musical feel of some of her early work, and, it is whispered, because of an allusion in the last verse, to a queen 'who plays guitar and cries and sings'. The lyrics convey a yearning for the good life in California as the narrator takes his chances on a big jet plane, going to look for a girl out there 'with love in her eyes and flowers in her hair'. In later years, Plant said that the song might have been a little embarrassing, but it summed a period of his life when he was only aged twenty-two, struggling to find himself 'in the midst of all the craziness of California and the band and the groupies'.

Live, it became a regular feature of their acoustic sets, from the British spring 1971 tour onwards, and also during Plant's solo tours from 1988 onwards, at Page and Plant's 1990 Knebworth appearance, and on their 1995–98 world tours.

8. 'When the Levee Breaks' (Bonham, Jones, Memphis Minnie, Page, Plant) 7.08

On the second longest track on the album, the group returned to their blues roots with a number first recorded by duo Wilbur 'Kansas Joe' McCoy and Memphis Minnie in 1929. It told the story of a severe flood throughout the state of Mississippi and surrounding areas that destroyed homes and devastated the local agricultural economy, forcing many people to the Midwest in search of work. It inspired a number of songs, this particular one telling how more than 13,000 residents in and around Greenville made for a nearby, unaffected embankment on high ground for shelter. The group recorded an initial version in December 1970, later released as 'If it Keeps on Raining' on the 2015 reissue of *Coda*, but the one which closes the fourth album was a second effort taped in May 1971.

Page and engineer Andy Johns devised a novel way of recording Bonham's drums by placing him and his new Ludwig kit at the bottom of a stairwell at Headley Grange, then using two microphones at the top to create a distinctive resonant, slightly muffled sound. Plant's harmonica part was recorded using a backward echo technique and phasing was applied to some of the vocals. Page was particularly proud of the 'super-dense sound in layers' built around the drum track. For him, it was probably the most subtle thing on the whole album because of all the different effects that he had never used before.

Because of the production techniques used in the studio, they found it hard to play live to their satisfaction, only performing it on stage a few times on the early dates of their American tour in 1975, and then not again until they were inducted into the Rock and Roll Hall of Fame twenty years after that, with a guest appearance from Neil Young and Michael Lee on drums. Page and Plant included it in *Unledded* and on their 1995–96 world tour.

5

House of the Holy

UK: released 26 March 1973, Atlantic, No. 1 for two weeks (2015 reissue, No. 34)
US: released 18 March 1973, Atlantic, No. 1 for two weeks
Current edition: Atlantic CD
Personnel: Robert Plant—lead vocals
Jimmy Page—electric, acoustic and pedal steel guitars, Theremin
John Paul Jones—bass guitar, keyboards, clavinet, synthesizer bass, backing
John Bonham—drums, backing vocals
Recorded at Rolling Stones Mobile Studio, Stargroves, and Headley Grange, Hampshire; Island Studios, London; Electric Lady Studios, New York, December 1971–August 1972
Produced by Jimmy Page

Most of the group's fifth album was recorded at the end of 1971 and in the early months of 1972 with the Rolling Stones Mobile Studio at Stargroves and Headley Grange, Island, and Olympic Studios. They aimed to release it in June 1972 in time for the American tour, on which some of the material was previewed with Plant announcing from the stage that it would be called *Burn That Candle*. Dissatisfied with the results, Page decided more work was necessary, so further recording and overdubbing was undertaken in New York. Several songs started as demos at the home studios that Page and Jones had recently installed so they could complete arrangements begun with the group earlier, Page supervising 'The Rain Song' and 'Over the Hills and Far Away', and Jones 'No Quarter'. Four additional songs, 'Houses of the Holy', 'Black Country Woman', 'Walter's Walk', and 'The Rover', were held over for release on subsequent albums. It was ironic that the first Led Zeppelin album to have a title other than a number was named after a track that did not appear on it but on its successor, yet they thought 'Houses' sounded too similar to 'Dancing Days'.

On a musical level, it saw a change in that the group were departing from their blues influence, experimenting as they worked in more contemporary styles, particularly funk and reggae, at the risk of alienating some fans who just wanted more of the same instead of a more eclectic Led Zeppelin. In retrospect, it is one of the less well-regarded albums in their canon. Too much of the unexpected, not enough of the hard blues rocking that established them, and two semi-jokes, 'The Crunge' and 'D'yer Maker', suggested they were not exactly on peak form. Moreover, while the tilt towards acoustic music on the third album still had one foot firmly in the blues, much of the fifth did not. Others regard it as a more adventurous work by a group less insistent on proving themselves, cutting loose, and having fun.

For the second album in a row, they resisted demands to print the title, their name, Atlantic logo, or catalogue number on the sleeve on the grounds that it would compromise the integrity of the artwork, a panoramic image of two small naked children climbing the Giant's Causeway in Northern Ireland. Grant's compromise—that a paper wrapper around the sleeve bearing the title—was accepted. A break with tradition came in that the inner sleeve featured the lyrics to each song.

Entering the British album chart at No. 1, it stayed there for two weeks.

A remastered version was reissued in October 2014 in six formats: a standard CD edition, a deluxe two-CD edition, a standard LP version, a deluxe two-LP version, a super deluxe two-CD plus two-LP version with a hardback book, and as high-resolution 96k/24-bit digital downloads. The deluxe and super deluxe editions feature bonus material, alternate mixes or versions of every track apart from 'D'yer Maker', but no previously unissued songs. The reissue was released with an inverted colour version of the original album artwork as the cover of the bonus disc.

Tracks

1. 'The Song Remains the Same' (Page, Plant) 5.32

The opening track started as an instrumental by Page, with the working title 'The Overture'. Robert, he said later, had other ideas, along the lines of 'This is pretty good, better get some lyrics—quick!' He had the basic idea, and Plant suggested that they break down into half-time in the middle. After the ninety-second intro, as the vocal comes in, it slows down for about a minute before reverting to the previous faster tempo. Plant's lyrics are based on his belief that music was universal, on the theme that he had been around the world, from California to Calcutta, 'and at the root of it there's a common denominator for everybody'—it had the same power to move people wherever he was. For a while, it known as 'The Campaign' before being given its final title.

The vocal track was slightly sped up after being recorded, while Page used a Telecaster, multi-tracked, and a Fender twelve-string guitar. He, Jones, and Bonham are all playing quite a funky rhythm, something that was beginning to creep increasingly into rock music and would become more evident within the next two or three years.

It was first performed live on the group's 1972 Japanese tour. Bootlegs suggest that at the time it did not yet have an official title, and Plant used to introduce it on stage as 'Zep'. Played regularly at concerts over the next three years, it always went straight into 'The Rain Song', as it did on the album, with Page playing his Gibson EDS-1275 double-necked guitar. When they recorded their movie and accompanying soundtrack album, the song gave the project its title. It was also the opening number on the 1977 American tour and 1979 shows, but dropped from the set list on the final European tour, only to reappear at the reunion show in December 2007.

A 'Guitar Overdub Reference Mix' of similar length was included on the second disc of the remastered deluxe edition of the album, thus revealing how it would probably have sounded had they adhered to their original plan of making it an instrumental.

2. 'The Rain Song' (Page, Plant) 7.39

A seven-minute ballad and the longest track on the album, this was based on a melody created by Page at his Plumpton home, where he had installed a studio mixing console, consisting partly of the one that had belonged to the Pye Mobile Studio used to record their 1970 performance at the Royal Albert Hall. George Harrison, an avid fan of the group, was partly responsible for the inspiration, after a conversation with Bonham one evening when he told him that 'the problem with you guys is that you never do ballads'. Page responded to the challenge, saying, 'I'll give him a ballad', and even quoting 'Something' in the first two chords.[1]

Page brought in a full arrangement of the melody to which Plant wrote the words. It had a working title of 'Slush', a reference to its easy listening simulated orchestral arrangement. Plant ranked his vocal performance on the track as his favourite on any of their albums. Page plays a Danelectro guitar, Jones Mellotron, and Bonham uses brushes on the drums.

During tours between 1972 and 1975, the group played the first two tracks from the album in succession without a break, as Page played his Gibson EDS-1275 double-neck guitar on both, using the twelve-string on the first and the six-string on the second. Omitted on the 1977 American tour, it returned to the set list on their 1979 dates and again on the 1980 European tour when it was the only song they performed from the album.

A different version, similar to the original but without the piano is featured on the second disc of the remastered deluxe edition, titled 'The Rain Song (Mix Minus Piano)'.

3. 'Over the Hills and Far Away' (Page, Plant) 4.50

One of the songs that Page and Plant began work on in 1970 at Bron-Yr-Aur in 1970, the music was inspired by Page's Celtic ancestry. At one stage, it had the working title 'Many, Many Times'. Once again, when writing the lyrics, Plant referred back to his fascination with Tolkien, particularly the author's poem 'Over Old Hills and Far Away', published in 1915. However, his lyrics, which are far shorter than the poem, have more of a romantic element than Tolkien's poem, which describes a brief vision of 'Tinfang Warble', a magical dancing figure.

The introduction lasts for the first fifty seconds or so, with Page playing a six-string acoustic guitar, repeated on a twelve-string acoustic guitar in unison, adapted from the instrumental 'White Summer' (see p. 113). Plant's vocals then begin and the song continues briefly in folksy, Joni Mitchell-like mode until ninety seconds in, after which electric guitar, drums, and bass guitar take the song into a heavier direction. A couple of minutes of more funky rhythm ensue, culminating in a false fade, followed by an additional forty seconds of echo from electric guitar and a few chords played on harpsichord from Jones, plus a snatch on synthesiser in imitation of a pedal steel guitar.

Released as a single in America, it reached No. 51. It was premiered on the 1972 tour, almost a year in advance of release, and remained in the show up to the 1979 Copenhagen and Knebworth dates, featuring an extended guitar solo. Page played it on his 1988 solo tour, and he and Plant several times on their 1995–96 itinerary.

4. 'The Crunge' (Bonham, Jones, Page, Plant) 3.17

Evolving from a jam session in the studio at Stargroves, this opens with Bonham's drums laying down a funky beat with Jones adding bass and Page a riff on Fender Stratocaster, stepping on and off the beat in a deliberate effort to make it quite un-danceable. Plant then starts improvising lyrics about his obsession with the girl next door. There is also a reference to Otis Redding and one, if not two, of his songs in the line 'Ain't gonna call me Mr Pitiful, no I don't need no respect from nobody'. Yet the main inspiration here was James Brown, many of whose earlier studio recordings were improvised with little or no rehearsal time, so he would call out directions to the musicians such as 'take it to the bridge' (of the song). Towards the end of what is the shortest track on the album at just over three minutes, Plant calls out, 'Excuse me, oh will you excuse me, I'm just trying to find the bridge ... has anybody seen the bridge ... where's that confounded bridge?' It then ends abruptly.

They accordingly named it 'The Crunge' as a joke, and at one time, they planned to put a series of 'dance steps' as an illustration on the sleeve. Some fans saw and applauded the light-hearted side of it, while others thought it a piece of filler that suggested they were running out of ideas and it should perhaps have been left in the vaults.

As one of the most spontaneous studio tracks they ever cut, parts were generally heard in live concerts as part of a medley, often with 'Whole Lotta Love' and 'Dazed and Confused', or else a jam linking 'Whole Lotta Love' and 'Black Dog'. The drum intro, alongside parts of several records (by other artists), was sampled by De La Soul on 'The Magic Number', a No. 7 hit in 1990.

5. 'Dancing Days' (Page, Plant) 3.43

Inspired by an Indian tune that Page and Plant heard while in Bombay, hence the Eastern flavour to Page's guitar riff that opens the song, this was one of the group's most infectious numbers of all. Plant sings a carefree, uplifting lyric about dancing days being here again 'as the summer evenings grow' and a line that is almost pure early Chuck Berry, 'I told your mama I'd get you home but I didn't tell her I had no car'. According to engineer Eddie Kramer, when they heard the playback after recording it at Stargroves, they were literally dancing on the lawn outside with joy. The riff was later sampled by Bobby Brown on his 1992 single 'Humpin' Around'.

In March 1973, it was the first track from the album to be broadcast, when premiered by Emperor Rosko on his BBC Radio 1 lunchtime show. It was a regular feature in the set list on the 1972 tour, although rarely played thereafter except sometimes in an acoustic medley with 'Bron-Yr-Aur Stomp' on the 1977 American dates.

6. 'D'yer Maker' (Bonham, Jones, Page, Plant) 4.22

As on 'The Crunge', the group were just having a laugh. At a rehearsal one day, Bonham began playing a 1950s doo-wop-style rhythm, then started playing off the beat. From there, Page and Jones spontaneously broke into a mixture of reggae, dub, and an old late 1950s-type song, in the vein of Ricky Nelson or Ben E. King, with Plant ad-libbing lyrics over the top. The drum sound was achieved by placing three microphones some distance away from the kit. As for the title, that was adapted from an old joke: 'My wife went to the West Indies.' 'Jamaica?' ('D'yer Maker?') 'No, she went of her own free will'.

It is fair to assume that most people got the jest sooner or later, although before Bob Marley & the Wailers found mass acceptance, many British rock fans had regarded reggae singles as pop novelties and the whole genre as almost beneath contempt. One disgruntled fan was prompted to ask 'Any truth in the "Dandy Livingstone [a West Indian artist then enjoying regular British chart success] for Zeppelin rumour?"' on the *NME* letters page after hearing the track regularly on radio.

It was released as a single in America and reached No. 20. In Britain, Atlantic distributed promotional 45 rpm 7″ copies to the media and it was played regularly on Radio 1 and Radio Luxembourg 208 for a while, leading listeners to believe that it had been made available for general release. Plant was particularly keen for them to break the embargo on singles in their homeland but was outvoted, with Jones being the least enthusiastic. Much as he liked reggae, for him, it simply did not work and remained no more than a studio joke that misfired. According to him, Bonham was also totally unenthusiastic, especially as he hated playing reggae. When they were playing or messing around with the track, he found it really boring and would not play anything but the same shuffle beat all the way through. The whole point of reggae, Jones said, was that the drums and bass had to be very strict about what they played. Bonham would not, 'so it sounded dreadful'.

A note on the inner sleeve of early pressings of the album underneath the lyric asked 'Whatever happened to Rosie and the Originals?'—an American doo-wop group of the 1960s. Plant was happy to regard the song as a joke, and was amused when fans ignored the apostrophes (or else made fun) of the title and called it 'Dire Maker'.

Once it was apparent that the group were not going to sanction a full British single release, the public was given a choice of buying a more lightweight pop-reggae retread by Betty Joe, who according to those in the know is or was 'a session singer who needs to remain a bit of a mystery'. It was the only record ever issued under that name, and lack of airplay denied it any chance of success.

It made a brief appearance in concerts with a few lines being performed during the 'Whole Lotta Love' medley on the 1973 European tour, and in 'Communication Breakdown' at the final Earl's Court show in May 1975. The group never played it on its own, presumably as two of them at least regarded it as one of their less memorable efforts.

7. 'No Quarter' (Jones, Page, Plant) 7.00

This is Jones's most individual moment on the album, and hailed by some as his finest track with the group ever, an almost ambient seven-minute opus that is swamped in electronic treatments. His sometimes stark, sometimes bubbling keyboards and piano are the backbone of the whole piece, with Page contributing a jazzy solo and Bonham's drums contributing from time to time. Plant's lyrics tell of men coming home from war in a northern country, perhaps in another reference to Viking or Celtic legends, with lines such as 'The winds of Thor are blowing cold', and 'The dogs of doom are howling more'. They are in keeping with the title, a reference to showing no mercy to an opponent defeated in war. His almost unearthly cries towards the end contribute to a strange feeling of other-worldliness.

Although very much a studio creation that would have been difficult to reproduce on stage, it was regularly featured in shows from 1973 up to the 1979 Knebworth shows, in a lengthy version that gave Jones full rein to play some classical pieces as well on a Steinway B-211 grand piano. Among them were Joaquin Rodrigo's *Concierto de Aranjuez* and pieces by Rachmaninoff. Sometimes these would last up to thirty minutes or more, with the classical section acting as a bridge before turning into a blues jam, ending up with Page's guitar solo. At a show at the LA Forum in March 1975, they (or rather Page, Jones, and Bonham) played it as an extended jazz improvisation. On four occasions during the 1977 American tour, they used it to include a full version of B. Bumble and the Stingers' mock-classical 'Nut Rocker'. Though it was dropped from the set list on their 1980 European tour, Page and Plant featured it in *Unledded* and on their subsequent 1995–96 dates. Jones revived it in an instrumental version on his 1999 tour, while Plant used it to open the set when playing live with Strange Sensation in 2005, and two years later, it received another airing at the O2 Arena show.

8. 'The Ocean' (Bonham, Jones, Page, Plant) 4.31

A strange conclusion to an album that has already had its share of quirky moments, this begins with Bonham counting them in: 'We've done four already but now we're steady and then they went 1, 2, 3, 4'. A sturdy, even menacing guitar riff introduces the song in which Plant sings 'about the good things and the sun that lights the day, I used to sing on the mountains, has the ocean lost its way'. It is a rather grandiose and, at the same time, celebratory lyric, with the ocean being used as a metaphor for the sea of heads he used to see while he was on stage. Just over two minutes in comes a twenty-second lull with a few *a cappella* 'la la la' vocals, before the guitar riff comes in again. A little variation in tempo, from the staccato, funky riff to a bluesy swing comes in later on, and towards the end of the last verse is a reference to 'the girl who won my heart', his daughter, Carmen, who was three years old when they recorded it. A close listen, probably best on headphones, during the lead break will reveal the faint sound of a telephone.

It was a regular feature in the set list onstage throughout 1972 and 1973 but then dropped. Someone else did not forget it so easily. When Plant was taken to a Greek hospital after his severe car accident in August 1975, he was lying on his bed in considerable pain, trying to remove cockroaches from the bed. A drunken soldier lying in the bed next to him waved at him and started singing 'The Ocean'. Page used the riff on his version of 'Custard Pie' when played on the 1988 *Outrider* tour.

6

Swan Song Records

Led Zeppelin launched their label, Swan Song, on 10 May 1974. With manager Peter Grant as President, and offices in Kings Road, London, and Madison Avenue, New York, it was intended as a vehicle for the group to release their own material and also sign artists in whom they believed and who were finding it hard to sign with other major labels. It was a move that a select few other acts had made with varying success over the previous six years, notably The Beatles, Rolling Stones, Deep Purple, Moody Blues, and Elton John. After their five-year contract with Atlantic expired at the end of 1973, they were free to make plans to do so, although Atlantic continued to distribute all releases. The distinctive design was based on the central figure in *Evening: Fall of Day*, a painting by nineteenth-century American artist William Rimmer.

In addition to Led Zeppelin themselves (as a group, and subsequently Page and Plant as solo artists), the artists whose records appeared on the label were The Pretty Things, Dave Edmunds, Detective, Wildlife, Maggie Bell (and her group Midnight Flyer, plus a duet she recorded with B. A. Robertson), and Bad Company, although the latter were signed to Island in Britain until 1979. Of the twenty-seven singles released in Britain (excluding Led Zeppelin's promotional only 'Trampled Underfoot'), Edmunds accounted for thirteen, including the only one that ever reached the Top 10, the Elvis Costello-penned 'Girls Talk'. Of the eighteen albums, five were by Led Zeppelin plus one solo project by Plant and one by Page, and another five by Edmunds, one of which was a 'best of' compilation.

It ceased operations in October 1983, with subsequent Led Zeppelin compilations and live albums being released on Atlantic again.

7

Physical Graffiti

UK: released 24 February 1975, Swan Song, No. 1 for one week (2015 reissue, No. 6)
US: released 24 February 1975, Atlantic, No. 1 for six weeks
Current edition: Swan Song CD
Personnel: Robert Plant—lead vocals, harmonica, acoustic guitar
Jimmy Page—electric, acoustic, lap steel and slide guitars, sitar, mandolin
John Paul Jones—bass guitar, organ, acoustic and electric piano, Mellotron, guitar, mandolin, VCS3 synthesiser, Hohner clavinet, Hammond organ, string arrangements
John Bonham—drums, percussion
Ian Stewart—piano (track 13)
Oman Karniparinpil—Jew's harp (track 6)
Recorded at various studios including Headley Grange and Olympic, July 1970, December 1970-March 1971, May 1972, January–February 1974
Produced by Jimmy Page

For the group's first album to be released on their own label, they began writing and recording new songs using Ronnie Lane's Mobile Studio at Headley Grange in November 1973. After a break over the Christmas holiday, sessions resumed in the new year when they recorded eight tracks at Headley Grange in January and February 1974. In Plant's words, they 'did some real belters with live vocals, off-the-wall stuff that turned out really nice'. The informality of their surroundings gave them an opportunity to improvise and develop new material.

As they soon found they had more than enough for one disc, they decided to make it a double album by adding unreleased material from previous sessions, using one outtake from the third, plus three from the two subsequent releases, figuring 'it was better to stretch out than to leave off'. Maybe they had in mind the example of The Beatles, whose 'white album' in 1968 was their first double as well as their first on their own Apple label. According to their engineer Ron Nevison, the decision to expand it thus was not part of the original planning. He left the project before they started reworking older material and never knew it was going to be a double until it was released. After additional overdubs, final mixing was performed in October 1974 at Olympic Studios. The title was coined by Page as a way of illustrating the physical and written energy that he had put into producing.

Having been let loose on four sides of vinyl instead of two, they savoured the luxury of an album that demonstrated every facet, every style of their repertoire. For once, they could indulge in the more experimental, less typical styles as seen on the previous record, as well as giving fans what they expected and seemed to prefer. Containing recordings made over a timespan of almost four years out of their (at the time of release) six-year career, it includes hard rock, eastern-influenced orchestral material, progressive rock, driving funk, acoustic rock 'n' roll, love balladry, blues, country rock, and an acoustic guitar instrumental. It contains both the longest and shortest studio recordings they ever released, from eleven minutes to just over two, and also features Jones playing additional guitar on several tracks, something he had only done on one track on the fourth album and would never do again. After they disbanded, Plant singled it out as his favourite, the one that represented them at their most creative, while for Page, it was their 'high-water mark'.

If 'Houses of the Holy' had been a mild disappointment for some, its successor saw them back at full throttle. Like other double albums of the era by rock's first division names, from Bob Dylan's *Blonde on Blonde* to The Beatles' eponymous 'white album', from The Rolling Stones' *Exile on Main Street* to ELO's *Out of the Blue*, it was a vast tapestry, a garden of aural delights, with room for the expected but hard rocking more-of-the-same, blues, funk, pop, rock 'n' roll, plus a foot in the more experimental-and-diverse camp, the ultra-short and the ultra-long. No fan could ask for more.

The original die-cut sleeve design showed a photograph of two five-storey buildings of a New York City tenement block, 96 and 98 St Mark's Place, through the windows of which a number of American cultural icons such as W. C. Fields, Lee Harvey Oswald, and Buzz Aldrin and the faces of the group are visible. It was the brainchild of Peter Corriston, an American graphic designer noted for his innovative record sleeves. Wanting a symmetrical building with interesting details, not obstructed by other objects and that would fit the square album cover, he and his team walked around the city for several weeks looking for the right building. The original album featured the building with the windows cut out on the cover and various sleeves that could be placed under the cover, filling the windows with the album title, track information or liner notes. Some details in the original photograph were altered so it would fit the square cover format.

A remastered version was reissued in February 2015, in six formats: a standard two-CD edition, a deluxe three-CD edition, a standard two-LP version, a deluxe three-LP version, a super deluxe three-CD plus three-LP version with a hardback book, and as high-resolution 96k/24-bit digital downloads. The deluxe and super deluxe editions feature bonus material containing alternative takes, three of which are different titles, 'Brandy and Coke' ('Trampled Under Foot'), 'Everybody Makes it Through' ('In The Light'), and 'Driving Through Kashmir' ('Kashmir').

Tracks

1. 'Custard Pie' (Page, Plant) 4.15

With a nod to the inspiration of songs from Sleepy John Estes, Blind Boy Fuller, Bukka White, and above all 'Custard Pie' by Sonny Terry & Brownie McGhee, the group started off the album with a number that owed something to the shuffling rhythm forever associated with Bo Diddley and also the much-covered Buddy Holly song 'Not Fade Away'. Plant ad-libbed the lyrics, based on lines from old blues standards and in keeping with the lascivious mood of the originals. Lines like 'Chewin' a piece of your custard pie' are nothing to do with pudding, but ample evidence that he could give people like George Formby, as well as the bluesmen, a run for their money when it came to double entendres.

A little less than halfway through, Page adds a wah-wah solo played through an ARP synthesiser, while Plant adds harmonica later on, and Jones plays clavinet as well as bass guitar.

Part of the song was played during their acoustic set during one of the American shows in May 1977, but they never performed it in its entirety. It was only granted a life on its own after the group had disbanded. Plant added a chorus on to the end of his song 'Tall Cool One' in live performances from 1988 onwards, while that same year, Page featured it on his *Outrider* tour. In 1990, it was played at Jason Bonham's wedding reception; five years later, Page and Plant performed it on their world tour, and Page brought it out for another airing on tour with The Black Crowes.

2. 'The Rover' (Page, Plant) 5.39

Written at Bron-Yr-Aur in 1970 and first recorded at Stargroves a couple of years later, this was initially intended as an acoustic number for the fifth album. It was then held over as Page wanted to work on it further, overdubbing it with electric guitars. The result was one of the musically heaviest numbers on the album, with just guitars, bass guitar, and drums behind the vocal. Plant's lyrics are about a wanderer who has seen London, the seven wonders, and 'the kings who rule them all' while his lover 'is lying on the dark side of the globe'.

In concerts, instrumental themes from the song featured in the 'Whole Lotta Love' medley on one of the Australasian concerts in 1972, and the opening bars were played as the introduction to 'Sick Again' on the 1977 tour, but the complete number was never played on stage. Part of it found its way into 'Babe I'm Gonna Leave You' when Page and Plant went on tour in 1995.

3. 'In My Time of Dying' (Bonham, Jones, Page, Plant) 11.05

At eleven minutes and five seconds, this holds the record for being their longest track on a studio album in terms of playing time. It had its origins in a traditional gospel song recorded in 1926 by Blind Willie Johnson, although earlier and later versions go under the title 'Jesus is Gonna Make up my Dying Bed' or minor variations on those words. Other blues artists such as Charley Patton and Josh White recorded versions not long afterwards, and it was one of several traditional songs to appear on Bob Dylan's first album, recorded in 1961. Being in the public domain, all four members were free to claim a joint writing credit.

As in the case of 'Whole Lotta Love', Michael Hann makes an eloquent argument against any accusations of plagiarism, pointing out that rock 'n' roll was built on a limited number of chords and a limited number of ways of deploying them. It was inevitable that the same words, only slightly rearranged, would occur in several different songs. While Led Zeppelin's 'borrowings were more craven than most', a comparison between their songs and the original recordings of older numbers from around forty years earlier soon reveals the major differences. Listening to Josh White's 'Jesus Gonna Make Up My Dying Bed' reveals 'a haunted, spooky acoustic blues' that admittedly bears a certain similarity to 'In My Time of Dying'. Yet when listening to the latter, 'you will hear an astonishing edifice of brutal power and terrifying force', which would not have existed without the older number song, but it is not a simple cover version, more an extrapolation or a reimagining of where it 'could have ended up'.[1] Mick Wall is another one of many to remind us that with folk and blues 'traditions' based on tunes handed down over generations, Page had just as much right as the earlier artists whose works also borrowed from others. Even songs by Bob Dylan and The Beatles were transparently derivative on occasion.[2]

On this song, Page used an open 'A' chord tuning on slide guitar, unaccompanied for the first forty-five seconds until the fretless bass guitar and drums join in, with vocals taking another twenty seconds after that. A reverb effect was used on the drums to create a heavier sound. Nearly four minutes in, a repeated guitar chord signals a faster section and it continues in this vein for another six minutes or so until Plant sings the final dramatic phrase after a concluding guitar chord. The tape was left running in the studio with his cough a few seconds later, followed by the sound of Bonham calling out, 'That's gotta be the one, hasn't it?' and someone else invites them to come and have a listen. Page left it in to reflect the relaxed time they had while recording. He explained later that they had a framework for the arrangement but then it just 'took off' and they were having a ball simply jamming.

They performed it on stage during the 1975 and 1977 tours, during which Plant generally dedicated it to Denis Healey, then British Chancellor of the Exchequer, at a time when they were among the first rank of rock musicians driven into tax exile from Britain by the financial policies of the Labour government. Plant's enthusiasm for singing it live understandably waned after his severe car crash on holiday during the summer of 1975, and even more after the loss of his small son two years later. Nevertheless, he included it on his 1993 American solo tour, and integrated a few lines into the 'Whole Lotta Love' medley on the 1995–96 tour with Page, and again into 'How Many More Times' on their 1998 jaunt. The group's performance at the O2 Arena show in December 2007 was regarded as one of the evening's highlights. Page also featured it regularly on his post-Zeppelin career, on the 1988 *Outrider* tour, with David Coverdale on their 1993 Japanese dates, and again six years later with The Black Crowes.

Among other artists to cover it in recent years were Soundgarden, who often performed it in concert. At a gig in Detroit in May 2017, their final song was their own composition 'Slaves and Bulldozers', to which vocalist Chris Cornell added the first few lines of 'In My Time of Dying'. Next morning, he was found dead in the bathroom of his hotel, having had a long history of depression and taken his own life a few hours after leaving the stage.

4. 'Houses of the Holy' (Page, Plant) 4.02

An optimistic, mid-tempo song, this had been completed by June 1972 and was originally planned as the title track of the previous album. Plant's lyrics refer to 'sacred' places where young adults have their sexual rites of passion such as drive-in movies, concert halls, and arenas, as made clear by the opening lines, 'Let me take you to the movies, can I take you to the show', and the subsequent 'Let me wander in your garden, and the seeds of love I'll sow'. Passing references elsewhere in the song to 'Satan's daughter' and 'Satan and man' helped to fuel suspicions as to the group's alleged interest in the occult.

Page used a Delta T digital delay unit on his guitar to create the layered guitar introduction and fade-out, and on a close listen, the squeak of Bonham's bass drum pedal can be heard, as well as (unusually for him) a cowbell.

It was never played live by the group, and had to wait until 2000 when Plant sang a few lines from it integrated with an arrangement of the Garnet Mimms song 'As Long as I Have You' while touring with The Priory of Brion in 2000, and then until 2010 when he performed it with the Band of Joy on a solo tour in 2010.

5. 'Trampled Under Foot' (Jones, Page, Plant) 5.36

The group had already flirted with funk on 'The Crunge', albeit more in a James Brown style. This time they went even further. The song had its roots in a jam session in 1972, based largely around a clavinet or electric clavichord riff by Jones, which he acknowledged was inspired by Stevie Wonder's 'Superstition', an American No. 1 in 1973, and by Billy Preston's instrumental 'Outa Space', a No. 2 hit there the previous year. Similarities might also be noticed with The Doobie Brothers' 'Long Train Runnin'', which made the American Top 10 also in 1973, and in a musical climate where the singles charts on both sides of the Atlantic were replete with a number of disco hits, the group had rarely sounded so contemporary. A reviewer in *Rolling Stone* opined that it reminded him of Kool and the Gang.

Plant's lyrics are very much in the vein of Robert Johnson's 'Terraplane Blues', a Terraplane being a classic car. They are full of analogies between motoring and sex, with references to 'pumping your gas', 'revving all night', and 'coming for a service every hundred miles'. The words of the title do not occur in the lyrics.

Although clavinet is the instrument most in evidence throughout the track, Page played wah-wah guitar and used reverse echo.

In America, it was a single, reaching No. 38 (Billboard) and No. 28 (Cashbox). Although it never found full release as a 45 7″ in Britain, 5,000 copies were pressed for a promotional campaign to try and ensure that record shops were carrying plenty of stock of the group's albums around the time of the Earl's Court shows in late spring 1975. For every twenty units of their back catalogue that were ordered, a retailer was supplied with one copy of the single to sell or use for promotion in any way they wanted. The catalogue number, DC-1-A and DC-1-B, was stamped in the run-outs on either side, and not on the record label. It was packaged in a custom black die-cut glossy paper Swan Song bag with 'Led Zeppelin Trampled Underfoot' (not 'Under Foot' as it appears on the label, and indeed everywhere else on albums and CDs) along the top, the Swan Song logo at the bottom, and 'Special Limited Edition' in the bottom right-hand corner. While still a collector's item, the quantities pressed still make it by far the most easily found British Led Zeppelin single.

A rough mix of the track with less overdubbing, 'Brandy & Coke' (Trampled Under Foot) [Initial Rough Mix], was released in February 2015 on iTunes as part of the remastering process of all the group's albums. The rest of the album was released a few days later.

The number was a regular part of their set list on concerts from 1975 to the final gig in Berlin in 1980, usually with additional long keyboard and guitar solos, and with Plant adding lyrics from 'Gallows Pole', rather than singing every verse. Plant played it on his 1988 *Now and Zen* tour, which included a guest appearance by Page one night onstage at Hammersmith. When they toured together in 1998, it was back on the set list, and Jones included it on his solo tour the following year. It was also part of their show at the O2 Arena in 2007.

6. 'Kashmir' (Bonham, Page, Plant) 8.28

If there was a track that threatened to rival or even eclipse 'Stairway to Heaven' as the group's favourite or quintessential number among fans, listeners, radio DJs, music journalists, and historians, it was the one originally called 'Driving to Kashmir'. In its match of lyrics, mood, and instrumentation, in the eyes (or ears) of many, this eight-minute epic was to become their crowning achievement, the one they would never surpass.

During one of the earliest sessions for the album, Page recorded a demo at Headley Grange with Bonham in November 1973 while they were waiting for the others to arrive. In the previous year, he and Plant had been to Bombay together where they worked with Indian musicians. Having owned a sitar for some time, Page had developed an interest in tonalities of Eastern music, or open tunings in which open strings of the guitar did not produce a tertian (major, minor, or variants of the same) chord, and Arabic music. Tuning his guitar to D-A-D-G-A-D to reflect the Middle Eastern, North African, and Indian music inspiration, he started with a riff and then employed Eastern lines underneath.

'What I had in my mind was the riff and the cascades, which is electric 12-string overdubs, but also brass on the final thing,' he recalled. 'I had thought of the riff in orchestral terms, with cellos doing it, and this cascading brass, for the different colours of the orchestra. I didn't know it would work, but I knew it ought to theoretically.' As he and Bonham were experimenting with some of the ideas he had built up, he was keen to try this one out. The drummer fell in love with the concept immediately:

> He loves the fact that he's back in the hall with this great drum sound and this hypnotic riff. We're just playing it over and over over again. And then it gets to the point where we do literally a take of it, and I start counting it out as far as the verses are going to be, and then I try the electric trails for the overdubs and it's exactly what I think it's going to be. And I know this thing is really majestic. Even with just the two of us and these simple overdubs.

The riff itself, like the old French song 'Frère Jacques', was a round, the kind of number that 'catches up with itself'. For Page, it created the challenge of making sure that every other element of the song reached the same standard: 'The riff was so good that you had to make sure whatever you did as the first change really holds up'.[3]

Plant wrote the lyrics shortly after the group's 1973 American tour, in an area he called the 'waste lands' of Southern Morocco, after what sometimes seemed to become a never-ending drive along the road from Tan-Tan just off the Atlantic coast. For him, it was 'a place where your mind can really dance and where your imagination is way open'. Although Kashmir itself was a long way away, in Asia, he explained in a later interview that the inspiration really came from the fact that the road went on and on and on, a single-track route cutting through the desert. Two miles to the east and west were ridges of sandstone, and to him it looked like he was driving down a channel along a seemingly endless dilapidated road. Lines like 'Oh, let the sun beat down upon my face, stars to fill my dreams, I am a traveller of both time and space, to be where I have been' convey something of the endless journey, yet a feeling of hope at the same time.

Bonham's drums were recorded through an Eventide Instant Phaser PS-101, and Plant said his drumming was the key to the song, as 'it was what he didn't do that made it work'. Grant heard an early demo made by Page and Bonham, and he thought it sounded 'a bit of a dirge'. They sent their tour manager Richard Cole to Southall to find a Pakistani orchestra, and once he had done so, Jones had the job of orchestrating the work for the string and horn sections, then added his Mellotron. To him, the secret of arranging successful keyboard string parts was to play only the parts that a real string section would play, in other words one line for the First Violins, one line for Second Violins, one for Violas, one for Cellos, and one for Basses. Surprisingly, unlike Bonham, in view of his arranging work, Jones does not receive a joint writer's credit.

In retrospect, Plant called it 'the definitive Led Zeppelin song' and one of his favourites as 'it possessed all the latent energy and power that wasn't heavy metal'. Years later, he told biographer Mick Wall that he wished they would be remembered for 'Kashmir' more than 'Stairway to Heaven': 'It's so right; there's nothing overblown, no vocal hysterics. Perfect Zeppelin'.[4] Page recognised as soon as the completed it that it had that magic spark: '… we knew that it was something that was so magnetic within itself, and you couldn't really describe what the quality was … it seemed so sort of ominous'.[5] In a radio interview some years later, Plant recalled:

> [It is] an amazing piece of music … and an incredible challenge.… Because of the time signature, the whole deal of the song is … not grandiose, but powerful. It required some kind of epithet, or abstract lyrical setting about

> the whole idea of life being an adventure and being a series of illuminated moments. But everything is not what you see. It was quite a task, because I couldn't sing it. It was like the song was bigger than me.[6]

In the process, it acquired some unlikely fans. The Sex Pistols may have professed to hate Zeppelin and all they stood for at first, but after Johnny Rotten reverted to his real name of John Lydon and subsequently formed Public Image Ltd, he was so keen for them to perform it on stage that he contacted Robert Plant for the lyrics, as he could not decipher them from the record. Plant gladly obliged, and PIL regularly used it to open their set—ironically, in an instrumental version. Other artists who have recorded and released their own versions include The Dixie Dregs, Australian-based revolving door supergroup The Party Boys (who released a four-minute version as a single in 1984), and English/Australian string quartet Bond.

The song inspired Freddie Mercury and Roger Taylor to write 'Innuendo', the title track of the last album Queen completed and released before Mercury's death in 1991, partly in memory of John Bonham, and a song with a similar epic, Eastern-sounding quality. At the memorial concert for Mercury at Wembley Stadium in April 1992, Plant performed 'Innuendo' with the three surviving members, integrating part of 'Kashmir', followed by a short version of 'Thank You' and 'Crazy Little Thing Called Love'. Battling influenza at the time, he was disappointed with the quality of his vocal and withheld permission for it to be used on the DVD of the show.

In 1998, it bizarrely came within a hair's breadth of topping the British charts, albeit in a very different form and under another title. A rap version, 'Come With Me', billed as by 'Puff Daddy featuring Jimmy Page', was featured on the soundtrack of the movie *Godzilla*, with Page playing guitar (recorded, by his own admission, down a phone line) and appearing in the video. Released as a single, it reached No. 2 in Britain and No. 4 in America, receiving a predictably mixed reception from fans. The arrangement went on to be used heavily as radio and TV background link music, particularly on *The X Factor*.

The album track in its original form also appeared in the chart as a download-only single in November 2007 for three weeks, with a peak position of No. 80.

It inevitably became a favourite in live shows, as one of the songs they simply could not omit from the set list, and was played by the group on every show from one in Rotterdam, January 1975, to the final gig at Berlin in July 1980. When they played it at Earl's Court in May 1975, Plant was aware that a well-known former employee of his, no longer driving him around Wolverhampton in his father's window cleaning van since becoming front man of Slade, was among the audience. From the stage, he announced, 'I see my ex-roadie's in tonight, Noddy Holder!' and proceeded to dedicate

'Kashmir' for him. 'Black Country humour,' said Holder.[7] Starting with the 1977 American tour dates, it led out of Page's solo spot on 'White Summer/ Black Mountain Side'. In 1988, it was included in their show for the Atlantic Records fortieth anniversary celebration, and that same year, on his *Outrider* tour, Page used a few riffs during his 'Moonlight Midnight' medley. Page and Plant performed it in their *Unledded* show and on their 1995–96 world tour, as well as releasing a twelve-minute version as a CD single in France. Twelve years later, it was generally considered the high point at their O2 Arena show, greeted with the loudest audience roar of the night. A review by Pete Paphides in *The Times* the next day noted that 'the moment Page and Bonham locked into "Kashmir" something transcendent took hold'.[8]

7. 'In the Light' (Jones, Page, Plant) 8.47

The song that launched side three of the original vinyl package, and the second longest at nearly nine minutes, is another eastern-sounding number. For the first hundred seconds or so, an intro played by Page's violin bow on an acoustic guitar producing a psychedelic drone to accompany Jones's synthesiser solo sets the mood. The drums and electric guitar join in another minute after that, and four minutes into the piece, a fanfare of stately baroque-style chords on clavinet and synthesiser, and descending bass line, lead to a striking guitar solo lasting about forty seconds before a return to the bagpipe-like drone of the intro. Jones was always particularly proud of this section, saying that his riffs could always be distinguished from those by Page—his had more notes and were linear, while Page's tended to be 'chunkier and chordier'. The pattern of stop-go drums carries on until the magnificently uplifting fadeout, with Page's multi-tracked guitar and delayed echo. Plant's lyrics are in shoulder to lean on, 'Reach Out I'll Be There' or 'You've Got a Friend' mode, with lines like 'And if you feel that you can't go on, and your will's sinking low ... In the light you will find the road ... Let me share your load'.

A slightly different version, 'Everybody Makes It Through (In the Light)' [Early Version/In Transit], about two minutes shorter, was recorded with alternate structure and lyrics, beginning 'Sunshine brings laughter, rainclouds bring me down', instead of 'And if you feel that you can't go on, and your will's sinkin' low'. This appeared on the deluxe version on 23 February 2015, a third CD including other outtakes and alternate mixes, as part of the remastering and reissue process of all nine albums. Yet another version appears on the deluxe reissue of *Coda* (see p. 117).

Page named it as his favourite track on the album. He said later that he 'had no idea at the time that John Paul Jones was going to come up with such an amazing synthesiser intro, plus there's all the bowed guitars at the beginning as well, to give the overall drone effect ... when he did that start, it was just unbelievable.'[9] In another interview, he referred to it as the follow-up to 'Stairway to Heaven'.

Plant also called it one of the group's finest moments ever. He was particularly keen to play it live, but they never managed to because Jones was unable to reproduce the synthesiser sound outside the studio. Post-Zeppelin, it was used as an intro link by Plant on some of his *Now and Zen* solo shows in 1988. He and Page played it on their tours between 1995 and 1998 as part of a medley with other songs, while Page played it in full with The Black Crowes in 2000, as did Plant while touring America and Scandinavia in 2001 with Strange Sensation.

8. 'Bron-Yr-Aur' (Page) 2.06

One of the longest tracks on the album is followed by the shortest of all. Recorded at Island Studios in May 1970 during sessions for the third album, it is also the oldest. An instrumental in the vein of Page's early heroes Bert Jansch and Davy Graham, written during his and Plant's sojourn in Wales that year, it features him finger-picking a Martin D-28 and an open C6 tuning, complete with occasionally squeaking strings.

It featured briefly as part of the group's acoustic set on the 1970 late summer American tour to promote the forthcoming album on which they were planning to include it, but was never played on stage again afterwards.

9. 'Down by the Seaside' (Page, Plant) 5.15

Originally written as an acoustic song at Bron-Yr-Aur in 1970, the group first recorded it a year later with an electric arrangement. It was planned for the fourth album but held over. The title's similarities to 'Down by the River', the country rock feel, and, above all, Plant's slightly nasal twang immediately call a Neil Young influence to mind. His lyrics alternate between a carefree atmosphere of watching the world go by as the boats are sailing, and the comic question 'Can the people hear what the little fish are saying?' with its overtones of anthropomorphism, and a less positive tones later on about how in the city streets, 'all the folk go racing, no time left to pass the time of day'.

Musically, Jones's Hohner electric piano and Page's pedal steel guitar sound, probably played through a Leslie speaker to create the underwater feel, help to create a gentle country atmosphere. About two minutes in, there is a grittier, more hard rocking section that lasts for about forty seconds before it reverts to the previous tempo. Towards the end, the guitar solo is interspersed with sunny vocal harmonies, reminiscent of The Beach Boys or even The Beatles *Sergeant Pepper*-era.

Plant had wanted to include this track on the third album but was voted down by the others, with Jones being particularly unenthusiastic. The group never played it live, but Plant always retained a particular fondness for the song. On a twelve-track Led Zeppelin tribute album, *Encomium*, by various artists and released in 1995, he recorded the song as a duet with Tori Amos, the only member of the group to appear on the whole record. He also featured some lines in one of their medleys while touring with Page in 1995–96.

10. 'Ten Years Gone' (Page, Plant) 6.34

Originally intending this to be an instrumental piece, Page used up to about fourteen guitar tracks to overdub the harmony section. The first forty seconds feature just one guitar—a second then joining in—that has been likened to The Beatles' 'Dear Prudence' and Paul McCartney's 'Band on the Run'. The vocals come in after about one minute. A medium-to-slow-paced piece of work, it relies on the tapestry of guitar sounds to build up to a brooding crescendo of sorts until five minutes in, when the bass and drums pause for twenty seconds to allow a solo guitar some space. All the instruments return for the final minute until it fades. The subtle tone differences in the guitar passages recall the menacing atmosphere of Fleetwood Mac's 'Green Manalishi'.

Plant's bittersweet lyrics are about an old flame who some ten years previously had made him choose between her and his musical career, telling him that it was either her or his fans: 'Kind of makes me feel sometimes, didn't have to grow, but as the eagle leaves the nest, it's got so far to go'. His response to her at the time, he said, was that he did not actually have any fans, but he had 'got to keep going'. He praised Page's construction of the track, remarking that it had been painstakingly pieced together from sections he had written and arranged in the studio.

Speculation that the song was a variation of an unreleased group recording, 'Swan Song', which gave them the title for their record label, has been given the lie by bootlegs of studio material that show how dissimilar both songs are.

The group performed it live on their 1977 American tour. Jones initially played an acoustic guitar until he was given a custom triple-necked instrument specially created by luthier and technician Andy Manson, comprising six-string and twelve-string guitars, a mandolin, and bass pedals. Page used a brown-painted 1953 Fender Telecaster, once nicknamed 'Botswana Brown' by a music journalist. They played it again on the first date of their Knebworth concerts in August 1979 but dropped it from the second because of problems with the sound system. Page and Plant performed it once on tour in Japan in 1996, and Page again with The Black Crowes in 1999 and 2000.

11. 'Night Flight' (Jones, Page, Plant) 3.38

Another of the older songs on the album, this was originally recorded by the group at Headley Grange in January 1971. Short and sweet, three and a half minutes long, it has the briefest of introductions—probably a couple of shuffles on Bonham's hi-hat—before Plant begins singing, and it reaches the end without a guitar solo. Page plays rhythm guitar through a Leslie speaker, while Jones adds Hammond organ. Plant's lyrics seem to tell of draft-dodging, a long train journey, and a Southern lady with 'a very special smile'. Jones was partly responsible for the music, and his Ian McLagan-like organ behind the Steve Marriott-style vocals bring The Small Faces very much to mind. Another recording was made with additional backing vocals.

Bootlegs are known of the group rehearsing it at a soundcheck at the Chicago Stadium in July 1973 during their American tour that summer, but it was never played live until Page and Plant performed it at a London show in October 1998, and Plant retained it in the set list with Strange Sensation while touring Scandinavia and America in 2001.

12. 'The Wanton Song' (Page, Plant) 4.08

Echoes of 'The Immigrant Song' kick off this gutsy number, with Page moving to and fro between two notes one octave apart again on the predominant riff. It developed from jamming at rehearsals, with a riff dominating the first minute, when a bridge shifts it with an oddly discordant chord into a different direction for about twenty-five seconds, then returns to the main riff, before taking up the bridge again. The guitar is again played through a Leslie speaker cabinet, with some use of backwards echo on the solo. Plant's vocals, as summed up by the title, are about having a good time with a 'silent woman in the night'.

Some years later, it was pointed out to Page (as if he was not already aware) that several of the group's songs did not have choruses. He replied that as far as he was concerned, the riff in 'The Wanton Song' was the chorus: 'It could go on for a half an hour and I would be completely riveted and satisfied. It's so powerful and concise that it never gets boring'.[10]

It was featured live on some of the American and European dates in 1975. Page and Plant revived it between 1995 and 1998, performing it on *Later with Jools Holland* on BBC TV in the latter year. Page also played it with The Black Crowes on tour in 2000 and on the *Jay Leno Tonight* TV show.

13. 'Boogie with Stu' (Bonham, Jones, Page, Plant, Ian Stewart, Mrs Valens) 3.52

Let your hair down, and everyone gather round the old pub piano. Never mind if it is out of tune. That was the feeling when this twelve-bar jam session was captured on tape on the Rolling Stones Mobile Studio at Headley Grange during sessions for the fourth album. 'Stu', Ian Stewart, was the Stones' road manager, and often tinkled the ivories on their records. He had been an original member of the group, until their manager Andrew Oldham decided he did not really look the part and relegated him to a backstage role. While Led Zeppelin were working on the fourth album in 1971 at Headley Grange, using the Stones' mobile recording unit, he was having fun on an old upright piano and Page was tuning his guitar to it—with, one assumes, some irony.

This track owed its very existence to the informal atmosphere at Headley Grange. Page recalled that some of the things they did there, like this number 'where Stu turns up and plays a piano that's totally unplayable, were incredible. That was too good to miss because Stu wouldn't record, he wouldn't do solo stuff. All of these things wouldn't end up on albums as far as other people were concerned, but they did with us.'[11] Somebody hit the record button as a jamming session began, and the result was a light-hearted helping of skiffle-influenced rock 'n' roll that sounds more like Mungo Jerry than Zeppelin. Unusually, Plant plays acoustic guitar, Page electric guitar, Jones bass guitar, and Bonham supplies a basic foot-stomping rhythm on the drums, perhaps with added tambourine, though other sources say that the slapping sound came from an overdubbed ARP guitar synthesiser. The guitars are far less in evidence than Page's solo—on mandolin.

The group's original working title for the number was 'Sloppy Drunk', although this was also the name of a song by Leroy Carr, a blues pianist and singer in the 1930s who died an alcoholic at the age of thirty. Plant's improvised vocals were based partly on Ritchie Valens' 'Ooh My Head', which itself was a thinly-disguised version of an older song by Little Richard, 'Ooh My Soul'. Page admitted that 'Robert did lean on that lyric [the Valens number] a bit', and as they knew that Connie Valens never received any royalties from the hits of her son who had been killed in the plane crash of 1959 that also claimed the lives of Buddy Holly and The Big Bopper, they decided to give her a joint credit along with all members of the group and Stewart. Despite this, Valens's publishing company, Kemo Music, later took legal action against them, resulting in an out-of-court settlement. As Page commented, 'So what happens? They tried to sue us for all of the song! We had to say bugger off!'[12]

14. 'Black Country Woman' (Page, Plant) 4.24

The loose spontaneous feel of the previous track spills over into this acoustic outtake from *Houses of the Holy*, an acoustic number taped in the back garden at Stargroves on a sunny day in April 1972. The first voice to be heard is Eddie Kramer: 'Shall we roll it Jimmy? We're rolling on what, one, no, one again.' (Cue sound of not-so-distant aeroplane ahead.) 'Don't want to get this airplane on.' 'Nah, leave it, yeah,' an amused Plant advises him. Sometimes they did not get off that lightly. On another occasion at the same place, he went outside to sing and was attacked by a flock of angry geese. Listeners who want to hear him swearing at a gaggle of disgruntled feathered session vocalists will comb the Zeppelin back catalogue in vain.

The song is another improvised twelve-bar blues sounding like a Leadbelly jug band stomper, with cheery if inconsequential lyrics on the theme of 'Hey hey, baby, why you treat me mean', with Page on acoustic guitar, Jones on mandolin, and Plant on harmonica. Bonham joins in on bass drum after about a minute, and on the full kit further on. The song was originally subtitled 'Never Ending Doubting Woman Blues'.

It was only played live once in its entirety, at Seattle on the American tour in June 1972, and thereafter as part of a medley with 'Bron-Yr-Aur Stomp' five years later, when Jones used an upright bass. Plant later sang it on his solo *Now and Zen* tour in 1988 and again almost twenty years later when touring *Raising Sand*, the album he recorded with Alison Krauss.

15. 'Sick Again' (Page, Plant) 4.42

At the end of the album, the group bow out with a scorching powerhouse rocker not far removed from vintage Rolling Stones. Page's chords, solos and backward echo-processed slide guitar sound every bit as menacing as Keith Richards in full cry, while Plant's vocals likewise have more than a touch of Mick Jagger about them, and Bonham's bass drum and fills match them to perfection. The final sounds after they finish playing are of slide guitar and a scrape of the plectrum against the strings, and a very faint cough from Bonham.

Ironically—whereas on several of the preceding tracks on the album, Plant's lyrics are more than a little lustful—on this number, he sings of the pity he feels for the adolescent girls who made a habit of flocking to the group's hotel rooms in order to offer them their favours, the 'painted ladies in the city of lies'. He sees them clutching pages from their teenage dream in the lobby of the Hotel Paradise through the circus of the LA Queen—'how fast you learn the downhill slide'.

It was performed regularly onstage during the 1975 and 1977 tour dates. During the latter, the group started it with the intro from 'The Rover', with Page using his Gibson EDS-1275 double-neck guitar. It was also in their set at Knebworth in 1979. Page played it with The Black Crowes in 1999–2000.

8

Presence

UK: released 5 April 1976, Swan Song, No. 1 for one week (2015 reissue, No. 10)
US: released 31 March 1976, Atlantic, No. 1 for two weeks
Current edition: Swan Song CD
Personnel: Robert Plant—lead vocals, harmonica
Jimmy Page—guitars
John Paul Jones—four- and eight-string bass guitars
John Bonham—drums, percussion
Recorded at Musicland Studios, Munich, November–December 1975
Produced by Jimmy Page

The seventh album was written and recorded at some speed after the group had to cancel a world tour following Plant's severe injuries in a car crash while on holiday in Rhodes. While convalescing, and at one stage fearing that with his broken ankle he might never walk again, he wrote several sets of lyrics, and worked on them with Page's music when the latter joined him at Malibu. Page, whose decision it had been to utilize their enforced downtime to full advantage, was the driving force, and his playing dominates the album throughout. The group rehearsed the material for a month at a studio in Hollywood, and in November 1975, they flew to Musicland Studios, Munich, with Plant still in his wheelchair. They had a tight schedule to meet as The Rolling Stones were about to record their next album there, and *Presence* was completed in eighteen days, their fastest recording turnaround time since the first album. Page had to stay awake for two days to complete all the guitar overdubs, which were done in one night. After the basic recording was completed, he and engineer Keith Harwood worked together for an average of eighteen to twenty hours per day while mixing everything until they fell asleep, then whoever woke up first would call the other so they could continue.

It was all finished on 26 November 1975, the day before Thanksgiving, and Page wanted to name it thus. In the end, they changed it in favour of a title that they thought would represent the powerful force and presence that they felt surrounded the group.

Six songs are Page and Plant compositions, the remaining one being credited to all four group members. After the more varied nature of the previous albums, with acoustic ballads and intricate arrangements, they (or rather Page) planned this as a return to hard rock, similar to their debut, except at a new level of complexity, and a change in their sound towards more straightforward, guitar-based jams and more simplified riffs. It was their only studio album without any keyboards (if Jones's piano on the deluxe edition bonus track '10 Ribs & All/Carrot Pod Pod' is not counted), and an acoustic guitar featured on the rhythm track of only one. A year elapsed between release and their return to touring, and only a minority of songs would ever be played live.

For Page, it was a delight to return to a less structured way of making music and completing an album in such a short space of time, commenting that there was a good deal of urgency and spontaneity about it. They had entered the studio with very little but a few ideas, and everything just came together. For him, it was their most important album, proving that they could still triumph against the odds. Some saw it as predominantly his project, with him in total control as he was on the first. Plant was also enthused at the time of release, saying his only alternative had been 'to turn around and stand against the storm with [his] teeth gritted and fists clenched and make an album'. He was pleased that it had taken so little time to complete, and about the unbending discipline they had shown while it was in the making. Nevertheless, it was an unhappy experience for him—working in a claustrophobic studio in the basement of an old hotel, missing his family badly, still recovering from his injuries, and convinced his strained vocal performance was well below his usual standard. For him, it would always be 'the wheelchair album', and it showed in his lyrics and vocals.

The general consensus among fans is that, after the richness of its predecessor, difficult circumstances combined with the lack of any top-drawer numbers apart from arguably the first, this, as a whole, was one of their lesser achievements.

The cover and inside sleeve, created by the Hipgnosis studio, features various images of people interacting with a black obelisk-shaped artefact. Inside the album sleeve, it is referred to as 'The Object', intended to represent the group's force and presence. The background used in the cover photograph is of an artificial marina installed inside Earl's Court Arena, London, for the annual Boat Show, the venue they had played in May 1975. The rear sleeve photo was taken during a summer break in a classroom in Westminster City

School, Victoria, London, where the wife of George Hardie, a member of the Hipgnosis team, was a teacher.

A remastered version, released in July 2015, comes in six formats: a standard CD edition, a deluxe two-CD edition, a standard LP version, a deluxe two-LP version, a super deluxe two-CD plus two-LP version with a hardback book, and as high-resolution 96k/24-bit digital downloads. The deluxe and super deluxe editions feature alternative mixes of four tracks, 'To Ones Are One' ('reference mix' of 'Achilles Last Stand'), 'For Your Life', 'Royal Orleans', and 'Hots on for Nowhere', and a previously unreleased instrumental, '10 Ribs & All/Carrot Pod Pod'.

Tracks

1. 'Achilles Last Stand' (Page, Plant) 10.30

The second of three studio tracks during their career that would break the ten-minute barrier opens the record. Plant's lyrics were written partly about his travelling through Morocco (where he and Page had gone shortly after the Earl's Court shows), Spain, and Greece, and by poetry he had been reading at the time, notably that of William Blake. The line from the song 'Albion remains, sleeping now to rise again' refers to an engraving by the poet and artist, *The Dance of Albion*, *c.* 1794, and the lines he appended below, 'Albion rose from where he labour'd at the Mill with Slaves, Giving himself for the Nations he danc'd the dance of Eternal Death'. A subsequent line in the song, 'The mighty arms of Atlas hold the heavens from the Earth', refers to the Atlas mountains in Morocco that look as though they are holding up the sky, as well as the giant Atlas who has to hold the world on his shoulders. The title is also an ironic allusion to Plant's last holiday (or last stand?) before it was recorded and while he was still physically fit.

Aiming to create something that, in his words, reflected the facade of a gothic building with layers of tracery and statues, Page's music took its cue from flamenco and Moroccan traditions. He applied vari-speed (variable speed pitch control) to make some of the guitar overdubs sound faster, giving the effect of different time signatures here and there. When the group originally rehearsed the number, it consisted of two sections. He was aiming for what he called 'an epic quality' so it would not sound like two sections repeated, something he could achieve by recording about a dozen guitar tracks to get the semi-orchestral arrangement:

> I knew it had to be jolly good, because the number was so long it just couldn't afford to be half-baked. It was all down to me how to do this. I had

> a lot of it mapped out in my mind, anyway, but to make a long story short, I did all the overdubs in one night.... I thought as far as I can value tying up that kind of emotion as a package and trying to convey it through two speakers, it was fairly successful.[1]

Because of the tight deadline to which the group were working, Page had to complete the track quickly, but this was not a problem:

> It was done in one evening, the whole of the arrangement. To be honest with you, the other guys didn't know: 'Has he gone mad? Does he know what he's doing?' But at the end of it, the picture became clear. It was like a little vignette, every time something comes around.[2]

Plant became so excited by what they were creating during the sessions for this track that he fell over in the studio and injured his ankle again. The original Achilles of Greek mythology, who unlike Atlas was not mentioned in the song's lyrics, had been dipped in the river Styx to make him immortal, but as his mother held him by the heel, it left him vulnerable. Paris then shot him during the Trojan War with an arrow through the heel. This legend provided them with the title for the number. Nevertheless, it was a harrowing experience for the singer, as the first track they worked on. The memory of the whole record, he recalled forty years later, was one 'absolutely wracked with pain [and] the fraternity of the band at the time stretched to breaking point'. On another occasion, long after they had disbanded, he played the song to a new girlfriend, telling her that if she wanted to know what he was like at the end of Zeppelin, this track would tell her. Having listened to it, she said she did not want to be left alone in a room with that: '"It's too much." That's what it was in the end: too much'.[3]

Jones plays a custom-built Alembic eight-string bass guitar. Bonham's drums help power the track with a distinctive shuffle, finishing with a final beat on the cymbals about forty seconds before the end, leaving Page to bring the number to a peaceful conclusion on guitar up to the fadeout.

This was one of only two tracks on the album, the other being 'Nobody's Fault But Mine', played regularly on stage by the group during their remaining concerts up to and including the 1980 tour. Page had originally planned to use his Gibson EDS-1275 double-neck guitar to play it live, but then found he could use his Gibson Les Paul or Fender Telecaster instead. On one of the 1977 shows, Keith Richards and Ronnie Wood came to see them. Richards told Page afterwards that he was rapidly becoming known as the most overworked guitarist in the business, and they needed another musician on stage. 'Quite amusing,' was Page's reaction. 'There are times when I'd just love to get another guitarist on, but it just wouldn't look right to the audience.'[4]

Page and Plant subsequently featured the song on their 1995 American tour. Page and Jones wanted to play it at the O2 Arena show twelve years later, but Plant allegedly blocked it on the grounds that the set should not be 'too heavy metal', or that he found it difficult to reach the high notes any more, thus dropping 'Immigrant Song' for the same reasons.

2. 'For Your Life' (Page, Plant) 6.25

According to Page, this was a relatively spontaneous number made up in the studio on the spot. Musically, it is one of their less adventurous cuts, one which uses a 1962 Lake Placid Fender Telecaster given to him by Gene Parsons, as he leads Jones and Bonham in laying down a solid, straightforward funk backing track. In that sense, it is comparable to Carlos Alomar's guitar track on David Bowie's 'Fame', an American No. 1 earlier in 1975, which might have been a subconscious influence. Towards the end, Page can be heard doing a few dive bombs on the tremolo arm of the instrument.

Written while he was confined to his wheelchair, frustrated at being kept so physically inactive, Plant's lyrics are an angry reflection on his observation of the heavy amount of cocaine that he feared was destroying the music scene in Los Angeles, as he blasted some of his peers in phrases like 'With the fine lines of the crystal payin' through your nose', and 'Down in the pits you go no lower, the next stop's underground'. Part of the song, he said, was also directed at a woman he knew who had been drawn into the local drug scene, and he was wagging a finger with the words 'watch it'. He regarded it as 'really like a sneering track, trying to tell everyone, "Now, you've got to look after yourself"'. Such words might well have been directed at somebody much closer to the group than that.

When Page teamed up with David Coverdale in 1993 and toured Japan together, they rehearsed the song but never played it live on stage. The group finally gave it its in-concert debut at the O2 Arena in December 2007, the only song played on that occasion that they had not previously performed live.

3. 'Royal Orleans' (Bonham, Jones, Page, Plant) 2.59

A second funky track in succession on the album suggests that the group must have been taking the rise of disco seriously at times, or at least listening to the likes of The Isley Brothers and Don Covay with at least half an ear. The subject matter is even more interesting, even if those involved cannot necessarily agree on the exact course of the events that inspired it. Phil Carson, head of the British division of Atlantic Records, said it was about one of the group waking up in bed in America with a drag queen, a story seconded by tour manager Richard Cole. While touring the States, the group used to stay at the

Royal Orleans Hotel, and one night, Jones brought a woman up from the bar, not knowing 'she' was not what he had supposed. After they had smoked a joint, they fell asleep, but one of the joints set fire to the bed. By the time they had woken up, someone had had to call the fire brigade, although nobody was injured.

Jones later disputed some but not all of the facts. Plant's lyrics slyly refer to 'John Cameron with Suzanna', how he kisses the whiskers, left and right, and later how he wakes up with a 'New Orleans queen' with a voice as deep as Barry White, the soul singer who was then at the peak of his success. Cameron is evidently the British musical arranger, whose main achievements included working on Donovan's 'Sunshine Superman' (on which Page and Jones had played in their session days) and helping to put CCS together.

This was the only track on the album credited to all four members. Plant had intended to make fun of Jones, evidently because the latter had once commented (presumably tongue-in-cheek) that vocals were the least important part of the group. Allowing him a joint writing credit evidently sugared the pill.

The stop-start-stop-start routine is accentuated by guitar and by Bonham adding bongos as well as his usual drums, while Page's solo is short and to the point, as is the song itself, being the only one on the album just shy of three minutes long.

It appeared on the B-side of 'Candy Store Rock' in America, France, Germany, and New Zealand.

To this date, none of the group have ever played it live. Maybe the subject matter hit a sore spot.

4. 'Nobody's Fault But Mine' (Page, Plant) 6.16

An old gospel song recorded by many musicians over the years, the first known was by Blind Willie Johnson in 1927, under the name 'It's Nobody's Fault but Mine'. When Plant said he wanted the group to do their own version, Page arranged it, but having been more familiar with a relatively recent recording by John Renbourn from the 1967 album *Another Monday*, owed little to the Johnson version. There was a theory that Plant was increasingly anxious about the group's misfortunes and the increasing drug use of Page and Bonham, desperate that his family had become victims of something that he might no longer be able to control. Lyrically, it has been called the group's own 'Hellhound on my Trail', a reference to the Robert Johnson song of 1937 that tells of a man trying to stay ahead of the evil pursuing him, but it does not address the cause or lasting solution for his predicament. References in the lyrics to addiction, 'A monkey on my back' and 'The devil he told me to roll, how to roll the line tonight', have been seen as a sort of exorcism.

Page triple-tracked his guitar intro, playing one guitar an octave higher than the others and using a phaser. At some points, the riff contains the same notes as and sounds like 'Whole Lotta Love', while Plant adds harmonica. There is a constant stop-start throughout the song.

The long lists of other artists who have recorded their own versions of the original song includes The Grateful Dead, Willie Nelson, Nina Simone, Tom Jones, John Renbourn, and, as a duo, Blues Band members Paul Jones and Dave Kelly.

It was part of the group's live set from the 1977 American tour onwards, at Knebworth and the final European tour. A close look at the film of the Knebworth show reveals Plant evidently spitting out the lines with some feeling. He featured it on his solo tours in 1988 and 1990, and in a blues/jug band arrangement with Page on the *Unledded* show in 1994 and the subsequent world tour. Page retained it while playing with The Black Crowes in 1999–2000. When the group played it at the O2 Arena in 2007, he joked that they first heard the song in a Mississippi church in 1932.

5. 'Candy Store Rock' (Page, Plant) 4.10

This is the only track on the album that includes acoustic guitar on the rhythm track, done in the style of a 1950s rock 'n' roll number, with Plant ad-libbing lyrics around the 'Ooh baby baby' phrase from 'Baby Let's Play House'. He probably had Elvis Presley very much in mind, especially as the latter had sent him a 'get well' telegram after hearing about the accident. The group shared the same American promoter, Jerry Weintraub, and had first met the king of rock 'n' roll after a show at the LA Forum in May 1974.

It only took them about an hour to write it, and the spontaneity comes across. Plant considers it one of his favourite songs on the album, and they released it as a single in America although it never charted, as well as in some European territories, Japan, and Australia.

It was never performed live except for a brief riff by Page at Riverfront Coliseum in Cincinnati, Ohio, on 20 April 1977. Page and Plant played a one-minute improvisation in concert as an introduction to 'Black Dog' on 26 July 1995 at Wembley Arena, and they also played it live in Montreux on 7 July 2001.

6. 'Hots on for Nowhere' (Page, Plant) 4.44

Similarities between this and 'Walter's Walk', particularly in Page's solo, a track recorded around 1972 and held over until the final album *Coda*, suggest that this was one of the tracks on which work had begun before the album sessions started. What sounds like a jaunty rockabilly tune is actually quite a bitter number, following the same theme as 'For Your Life'. Plant's lyrics are full of veiled allusions to Page and Grant, their increasing intake of recreational drugs, and the pressures they were putting him under while he was still far from fit and a long way from his family, his wife not being well enough to travel. 'When I learned how my time had been wasted, tear fell as I turned away' are the opening lines, while a little later he sings 'I've got friends who will give me fuck all', though his diction is perhaps deliberately less than clear, perhaps a ploy to avoid being banned on the radio. It was the only expletive ever used on any of the group's albums.

Page used a 1960 Fender Telecaster on the track. It was never played live on stage until Page performed it with The Black Crowes on their 2000 American tour.

7. 'Tea for One' (Page, Plant) 9.23

The song taking up the last nine and a half minutes marks a return to the group's slow blues roots, in a number that sounds similar to 'Since I've Been Loving You' on the third album. Page readily conceded that it was the only time they had ever really come close to repeating the mood of another of their songs, especially as the chordal structure was so similar. 'It was basically a 12-bar,' he said, 'and there were two verses to do as solos on guitar, and it suddenly hit me at that point that everybody has played a blues number, and there are so many musicians whose forte it is, like Eric Clapton, so what was I going to do?'[5] As they wanted to get a really laid-back blues feeling, he did two takes, one with a guitar solo, one without. He felt obliged to put a solo on but did not want 'to blast out the solo like a locomotive or something, because it wasn't conducive to the vibe of the rest of the track', but 'I was aware that you had to do something different than just some B. B. King licks'.[6]

As Page said, it was about 'ultimate loneliness in a hotel room', reflecting the vocalist's mood at the time. He felt homesick in America, away from his family, particularly at a time when the demands of the group had resulted in him working while he was still recovering from his injuries, sitting in a wheelchair and wondering 'is this rock 'n' roll thing really anything at all?'[7] The lyrics were written while he was sitting in a New York hotel, drinking tea for one. Lines like 'One minute seems like a lifetime, oh baby when I feel this way, sittin' lookin' at the clock' say it all.

A cover version has since been recorded by Joe Bonamassa, with Jason Bonham on drums.

Although never played live in its entirety, some parts of the guitar solo were incorporated into 'Since I've Been Loving You' at several shows from 1977. The actual song finally found its place in the set played by Page and Plant while touring Japan in 1996, where it received three airings backed by an orchestra.

Bonus Track

'10 Ribs & All/Carrot Pod Pod' ['Reference mix'] (Jones, Page) 6.49

Six and three quarter minutes long, this fairly slow piece presumably started life as a keyboard piece by Jones and was handed to Plant so he could write lyrics, but in this case, he never did, possibly through lack of time. As an instrumental, it has a very attractive quality, sounding more in line with the more carefully structured songs that made up most of the group's final album, and a little out of place alongside the rest of *Presence*. It starts as a stately piano solo, and no other instruments are heard until the guitar comes in sparingly two and a half minutes in. The drums, guitar, and bass all enter more solidly, albeit with restraint, another thirty seconds after that, with Page using acoustic and electric guitars, until it all comes to a graceful ending. There are hints of Steely Dan at their more laid-back and of the slower section of Elton John's 'Funeral for a Friend', and something of the delicate quality of 'All My Love' from the group's next album.

9

In Through the Out Door

UK: released 20 August 1979, Swan Song, No. 1 for two weeks (2015 reissue, No. 12)
US: released 15 August 1979, Swan Song, No. 1 for seven weeks
Current edition: Swan Song CD
Personnel: Robert Plant—lead vocals
Jimmy Page—electric and acoustic guitars, Gizmotron
John Paul Jones—bass guitar, mandolin, keyboards, Yamaha GX-1 synthesiser, piano
John Bonham—drums, percussion
Recorded at Polar Studios, Stockholm, November–December 1978
Produced by Jimmy Page

After the problems of their American tour in summer 1977, which culminated in cancellation of the remaining dates following the sudden death of Plant's son, Karac, the group took an extended break to allow him space and wait until he was ready to work again. Later he revealed that there were times when he did not really want to return to the group at all. After a period when all four members kept regularly in touch but were almost living separate lives, apart from a rather uncomfortable jamming session together in the spring of 1978, Plant finally felt prepared to commit himself to rehearsals and creating a new album in November. They recorded it over a three-week period at Polar Studios, Stockholm, jointly owned by two members of ABBA and their management.

Like *Presence*, the new album—and the one that, although they did not know at the time, would be their last—was created and recorded in difficult circumstances. Members of the group and their management had been beset by personal or health problems, some largely self-inflicted, during the last couple of years, with Plant and Jones annoyed by Page, Bonham, Grant, and tour manager Richard Cole's increasing alcohol and drug abuse. Page repeatedly had to quash rumours in the media that they were disbanding, and in a musical climate where punk and new wave groups had all the credibility while the *Saturday Night Fever* and *Grease* soundtracks were spearheading disco's domination of the British singles and album charts, Led Zeppelin were widely castigated as musical dinosaurs. The vocalist and bass guitarist, who had acquired 'a new toy', a Yamaha GX-1, would turn up to sessions promptly during the day, the drummer and guitarist probably not until the evening, so those who arrived punctually got on with the work in hand by working on brand new songs. Jones therefore had much more musical input this time, and two of the finished tracks became the first Zeppelin numbers on which Page received no writing credit. He did, however, produce and remix all the tracks at his home studio at Plumpton afterwards.

Three other songs, 'Wearing and Tearing', 'Ozone Baby' and 'Darlene', were recorded during the same sessions but dropped because of space constraints; they appeared on *Coda*.

Plant originally wanted to call the album *Tight but Loose*, but in the end, they said that trying to get back into the public mind was like 'trying to get in through the out door', hence the change of name. The outer sleeve, designed by Hipgnosis, comprised a plain brown paper bag, similar to bootleg albums with the title rubber-stamped on, and the inner sleeve featured monochrome artwork that, if washed with water, would become permanently fully coloured, like a child's painting book. There were six different designs, featuring a different pair of photos, one on each side, and the external brown paper cover prevented buyers from seeing which they were getting. The photo session in a London studio was arranged to look like the Old Absinthe House, New Orleans, with images all showing a scene in the bar, each being taken as seen by someone appearing in the other photos.

It was scheduled for release in Britain before the Knebworth concerts in August 1979, but production delays kept it from sale until later that month. Another transatlantic chart-topper, in America, it tied with *Led Zeppelin II* in staying at No. 1 longer than any of their other albums, and renewed American interest in the group, with all their previous albums returning to the Billboard 200 at the end of October 1979.

Three members of the group had their reservations about the record. Plant called it 'interesting but a bit sanitised because we hadn't been in the clamour and chaos for a long time ... more conscientious and less animal.'[1] For Page and Bonham, it had not been a 'comfortable' record to make, more 'a springboard for what could have been'. Others have seen it in retrospect as a more mature collection, the start of growing old gracefully, with Plant and Jones willing to experiment beyond the more guitar-dominated material that had always been Page's calling card.

At the time, critics and fans were divided. Some found the new synth-influenced music very contemporary while still retaining the dexterity and drive of their early work, while others either thought they had lost their way in moving from the heavier sound, or else not fulfilled their potential, sounding tired and unsure of themselves. The balance had shifted in that Page was not at his best at the time, and while in charge of production as ever, a failure to impose his personal vision on the project throughout meant that something of the spirit of the group was lacking. Now Jones had firmly impressed his stamp on this album more than the others, in terms of musical pigeonholing, it was more a progressive rock than a heavy rock album, with more than a nod to the likes of Emerson, Lake and Palmer, and Genesis. Page remarked that it was done in just over three weeks, and if he had really been in such bad shape as some people suggested, he would never have been able to play. His abiding memory of the Stockholm sessions was that the album took a different movement from the earlier ones, on which they were purposely trying to move away from the standard routine of ensuring that every track had a chorus. With hindsight, he felt that this one seemed to date quicker than its predecessors, 'but I don't want to take anything away from it.... We did some extraordinary singing and playing on it.'[2]

A remastered version was released in July 2015 in six formats: a standard CD edition, a deluxe two-CD edition, a standard LP version, a deluxe two-LP version, a super deluxe two-CD plus two-LP version with a hardback book, and as high-resolution 96k/24-bit digital downloads. The deluxe and super deluxe editions feature bonus material containing rough mixes of every track, four under different titles: 'Southbound Piano' ('South Bound Saurez'), 'The Epic' ('Carouselambra'), 'The Hook' ('All my Love'), and 'Blot' ('I'm Gonna Crawl'). The reissue was released with a grayscale version of the original album's artwork as the cover of the bonus disc, with a replica of the brown bag and the colourable drawing included.

Tracks

1. 'In the Evening' (Jones, Page, Plant) 6.53

The first track was the only piece with an overwhelming Page influence in its conception. It starts with about fifty seconds of a drone based around one note, a haunting evocation of Eastern sunsets and music, taken from a soundtrack he had been working on for Kenneth Anger's film *Lucifer Rising* (it may or may not have been coincidence that, two years later, the title track of ABBA's last album, *The Visitors*, opened the record with a similarly eerie forty-second drone). After that, Plant sings the title phrase, while a forthright guitar riff—for some critics, the only great Zeppelin guitar riff on the whole album—enters with Bonham's emphatic drums, which include a timpani as he plays long extended single stroke rolls and random single hits, changing the pitch of the drum with the foot pedal. Jones uses low sustaining bass pedals and Yamaha GX-1. As well as electric and slide electric guitar, Page uses a Gizmotron, a device invented by Lol Creme of 10cc using small motor driven plastic wheels to make the guitar strings vibrate and produce resonant synth-like effects from each string. It proved a simpler way of producing the sounds he had previously created with the bow. Thirty seconds before it fades out, the main guitar riff is briefly joined in unison by a phrase from Eric Clapton's solo from 'Outside Woman Blues', on Cream's second album *Disraeli Gears*.

Plant regarded this as one of the best tracks on the album, even though his lyrics are quite bitter, having as their theme how the rich and famous are exposed to suffering, albeit in different ways: 'All the pain that you go through, you can turn away from fortune, 'cause that's all that's left to you'. At least one commentator has noted that they are ostensibly directed at an unnamed woman, but the girl who shows 'no pity' could be the fickle mistress that is fortune.[3] To a casual listener, the oft-repeated line 'Oh, I need your love' could make it sound like just another pop song about romance.

It was featured on the group's 1979 and 1980 dates, with Page's guitar distortion and bowed solo accompanied by a laserstrobe to enhance the visual effects onstage. Later it became a regular fixture on Plant's 1988 *Now and Zen* solo tour, and he also performed it with Fairport Convention at the Cropredy Festival in 1992. It then became part of the set list on his tours with Page from 1995 onwards.

2. 'South Bound Saurez' (Jones, Plant) 4.13

One of only two songs by the group that Page had no part in writing, this is nothing less than a good-time, let your hair down rock 'n' roll tune. Jones's Jerry Lee Lewis-style piano (think 'Whole Lotta Shakin' Goin' On' but a little faster) colours the track throughout, with Page contributing a neat, suitably fiery solo about halfway through, while Plant's lyrics holding no deeper meaning than simply having a party. Never before had a Zeppelin track faded out with a straightforward 'sha-la-la' on the backing vocal.

It was never performed onstage, although as one of the most joyous, uncomplicated songs they ever recorded, it would surely have added to the atmosphere of any concert, especially if played near the end.

A mono mix was re-released in 2015 on the deluxe edition as 'Southbound Piano', the alteration perhaps an attempt to quell an ongoing debate about whether the second word should have been spelt 'Suarez' or not. If you google 'saurez', the first entry will tell you that the word means 'a party or reception held in the evening', and the only people who spell it thus instead of the French *soirée* are Led Zeppelin fans—all because of the apparent typographical error on the record. Will someone please pass the Spanish dictionary?

3. 'Fool in the Rain' (Jones, Page, Plant) 6.10

Jones and Plant developed the idea for the samba beat after they had watched the 1978 FIFA World Cup tournament in Argentina together, hence the start with a slightly Caribbean-style feel and keyboards dominating. Just over two minutes in comes a calypso section lasting about eighty seconds led by Bonham's Afro-Cuban drum patterns, underpinned by a reggae-inspired bass line. Their earlier collective effort on 'D'yer Maker' may have misfired, but this time round everything falls into place. Following this comes Page's solo in which he uses an MXR Blue Box effect pedal to produce the octave sound, and towards the end of his song he makes the bass riff a foundation for his guitar work at the end.

The lyrics tell of a man who is supposed to meet a woman on a certain street corner during a storm, and when she does not appear, he is filled with sorrow at being stood up. By the final verse, he realises that did not go to the right place for his rendezvous, making him 'just a fool waiting on the wrong block', yet with a twist in the line about redemption, or 'the love that I've found'.

It was their final American single, with 'Hot Dog' on the B-side, and reached No. 21 in February 1980, as well as being released thus in Canada, Mexico, several territories in South America, and Europe, New Zealand, and Japan. A radio edit of three minutes and twenty seconds was issued in America.

They never performed it live, but on 5 October 2005, Plant sang it with Pearl Jam at a benefit show for the victims of Hurricane Katrina that had devastated the Bahamas, Cuba, and much of eastern North America a few weeks earlier.

4. 'Hot Dog' (Page, Plant) 3.18

The only track not co-written by Jones, this is a rockabilly tune done in the style of a country hoedown, similar in style to 'Candy Store Rock' on the previous album. Influenced by Texas swing music, and also doubtless a tribute to early Elvis, it took shape during the group's London pre-production rehearsals, at which they often ran through a few 1950s rock 'n' roll songs while they were warming up. The song title refers to a distinctly American cuisine, although the words do not appear in the lyrics, telling the story of a man who has come into town to find his girlfriend, only to discover she has just taken the Greyhound bus and evidently left him. Some sources have said it is about Audrey Hamilton, a well-known Texan groupie of the time. Critics remain divided as to whether it is a genuine goodtime tune or lightweight throwaway, but it comes across as the most infectious, straightforward cut from their last phase.

Evidently inspired by the playing of Scotty Moore, which had influenced him in his teens, Page uses a Fender Telecaster on this song, outfitted with a

B-Bender, which raises the pitch of the guitar's 'B' string via interface with the musician's guitar strap, and is heard at the end of the guitar solo. Jones plays piano and mandolin as well as bass guitar.

It was performed live at the Knebworth shows in 1979 and on the 1980 European tour. During the two British concerts, according to some sources, Plant sang the last verse of the song with different lyrics to the studio version, ending with 'And I'll never go to Texas any more', instead of 'They just rolled my doll right out the door'. Others suggest less charitably that he either forgot the lyrics or just ad-libbed with less than his usual finesse. Whatever the truth of the matter, the group omitted it from the official DVD as they were dissatisfied with their performance.

5. 'Carouselambra' (Jones, Page, Plant) 10.34

At ten and a half minutes in length, in terms of playing time, this is second only to 'In My Time of Dying' as the longest song they ever recorded in the studio, dominated by Jones's Yamaha GX-1 synthesiser.

The name 'Carouselambra' is a reference to the keyboards on the first part of the song sounding like a carousel or merry-go-round, which reflects the musical atmosphere. Initially, it went under the working title of 'The Epic', developed during initial rehearsals for the album at Clearwell Castle in May 1978. Epic by name and epic by nature, it is a remarkably ambitious work comprising three distinct parts. Beginning with an intro sounding remarkably like The Stranglers' early singles, the first is a fast one given over largely to synths—the wizardry of ELP or Supertramp meets the carnival sound of Sailor—with Page's guitar less prominent than usual. The second, starting four and a half minutes in, is much slower, with full echo on the vocals and also highlighting Page's work, a deep, droning guitar sound produced with a Gizmotron based around two chords on a Gibson EDS-1275 double-necked guitar, the only time he used it on one of their studio songs. The song's concluding part, starting from seven minutes in, reverts to an up-tempo, more or less disco beat, with all four band members heard together, the bubbling keyboards being more dominant despite the odd fiery burst from guitar, for the final three minutes up to the fadeout (on reflection, an edit of the first four minutes might not have sounded out of place on an early 1980s dancefloor, sandwiched between Bee Gees or Chic hits of the time).

The vocals, particularly in the initial part, are buried too low for their own good in the mix and the words are thus not easy to decipher. Alternatively, make that 'impossible without reference to looking them up online'. It became a sore point with Plant, for he said that his lyrics were about a certain person who would eventually realise they were written about them, and ask, 'My God! Was it really like that?' His later comments suggested that he meant some of his bandmates, and possibly members of the management as well, as a veiled description of what had become their troubled creative chemistry in the later months. 'The whole story of Led Zeppelin in its latter years is in that song ... and I can't even hear the words!'[4] Yet he handled the matter with some subtlety, eschewing the blunt approach of, for example, John Lennon in his barely-disguised diatribe against Paul McCartney on the notorious 'How Do You Sleep' from his 1971 album *Imagine*, or some of the more transparently autobiographical, confessional lines by Ian Hunter in songs he wrote and recorded as a member of Mott The Hoople. Plant's lyrics are observations on some of what went on during the ill-fated 1977 American tour, yet couched in the poetical language that reflects his fascination with ancient historical legend.

Endeavouring to interpret some of the lines is almost like writing an A-level English Literature essay. The opening lines, 'Sisters of the wayside bide their time in quiet peace, await their place within the ring of calm', are a nod in the direction of the groupies that followed, while 'All was joy and hands were raised towards the sun' presumably a reference to the audiences of thousands watching them onstage. 'The storied hunter's eye' that sought out 'the unsuspecting and the weak' was presumably the heroin ensnaring certain members of the group and entourage and exhausting his patience. 'I heard the word, I couldn't stay' is assumed to be the reference to the call he received in July 1977 breaking the news of his son Karac's death, and 'They had to stay' is a reference to references to the fact that Page, Jones, and Grant stayed behind in America while only Bonham and Coles accompanied him back to England and attended the funeral with him. 'Where was your word, where did you go, where was your helping, where was your bow?' was presumably directed at Page for a similar reason. At the risk of idle speculation, such lines may be the reason why the guitarist deliberately obscured them in the course of mixing and final production. Significantly, a mono mix appeared in 2015 on the deluxe edition, under its original title 'The Epic', with much clearer vocals, and a slightly longer fadeout, adding about fifteen seconds extra.

Some fans and critics regard 'Carouselambra' as an unwieldy, overlong mess. The present writer begs to side with those who regard it as a bold, ambitious, adventurous, even almost symphonic work, which may be untypical Zeppelin—progressive rock, rather than heavy rock, for those who love to put music into neat categories—but very underestimated, overlooked, even one of the great unsung classics from their entire catalogue. For biographer Stephen Davis, it is 'like a ride on a fast, sinister merry-go-round, while the admittedly hard to make out lyrics 'had the cadences of a funeral oration for a Norse chieftain'.[5] All Music online acclaims it as 'quite possibly the definitive song from the underrated *In Through the Out Door* album in that it has key contributions from all members, especially Jones, and yet just isn't riff-dominated'.[6]

The music being very much Jones's conception, it was his idea that they should use the track as a centrepiece of their shows on the 1980 North American tour, which was cancelled when Bonham died. During the 1995–96 Page and Plant tour, the latter would sing the middle verse as part of their performance of 'In the Evening'.

6. 'All My Love' (Jones, Plant) 5.53

The second Jones-Plant collaboration on the album was surely the most tender song to which the group ever put their name. It is difficult to take issue with biographer Mick Wall's verdict that it is the most moving moment, 'musically, lyrically, emotionally', on which the vocalist 'simply opens up his broken heart and cries, as if directing the entire piece to his beloved son'.[7] The lyrics are nothing less than a tribute to his son, Karac, with evocative lines: 'Should I fall out of love, my fire in the light, to chase a feather in the wind?' As a song of bereavement or heartbreak in memory of a child lost before his time, it is on a level with Eric Clapton's equally poignant 'Tears in Heaven', a song about the death of his four-year-old son in an accident in 1991, on which the lyrics were begun by Clapton and completed by his writing partner Will Jennings. Plant's words are less direct and more shrouded in poetical allusion than those of Clapton and Jennings, inviting the listener to interpret them any way he or she wishes, although lines from the second verse—'The tides have caused the flame to dim, at last the arm is straight, the hand to the loom, is this to end or just begin?'—hint at the vocalist's determination to come to terms with his bereavement and move on.

Plant hardly needed to admit that his experience had left him a changed man. While he admitted that the album in general was 'not the greatest thing in the world', he stressed that they were trying to vary what they were doing, for the sake of their integrity. It was a little sanitised as they had been out of the 'clamour and chaos for a long time.... In 1977, when I lost my boy, I didn't really want to go swinging around—"Hey hey mama say the way you move" didn't really have a great deal of import anymore'.[8]

Jones's keyboards throughout are exquisite, taking centre stage in the break, which begins a little less than halfway through, with Page's acoustic and electric guitars contributing an equally wonderful few bars, but throughout the rest of the song never dominating proceedings. There is a slightly classical feel overall, with some comparing it to the more mellow work of ELO and Genesis. The final chorus before it fades out ends the song in a higher key.

Its working title was 'The Hook', and the rough mix on the deluxe reverts to that title. Outtakes on bootleg are known, one being about eight minutes long (two minutes more than the official version) with an additional synth solo, another with a proper ending as opposed to a fade, Plant extending the final chorus with more ad-libbing, and a twangy guitar solo by Page.

Because of the personal subject matter, Plant always regarded the song as one of the group's finest studio achievements. However, after the album was released, Page said he and Bonham talked about making the next album a return to the hard-driving, riff-based rock for which they had long been known, as they thought this 'was a little soft'. He cited this as the prime example, noting that he was not very keen on it: 'I was a little worried about the chorus. I could just imagine people doing the wave and all of that. And I thought, "That's not us." In its place it was fine, but I wouldn't have wanted to pursue that direction in the future'.[9]

It was only released as a single in some South American territories, being coupled in Argentina with 'Hot Dog' and in Peru with Herb Alpert's 'Rise' on the B-side. A promotional copy was issued in Brazil with a four-minute edit on both sides, one in mono and one in stereo. A cover version was released by Patti Boulaye early in 1980 as the B-side of her single 'I Know I'll Never Love This Way Again'.

The group performed it on all dates on their 1980 European tour and it was invariably well received. Plant also included several lines from it when performing the 'Calling to You/Whole Lotta Love' medleys while touring with Page in 1995–96, and Plant sang it on stage on his tour with Band of Joy in 2011.

7. 'I'm Gonna Crawl' (Jones, Page, Plant) 5.29

The group's last track on their final album is a return to the blues—a slow impassioned love song, almost in waltz time, in which Plant declares his love for a woman driving him crazy, the apple of his eye. Twenty seconds of prog-rock-style solo synth from Jones are followed by another twenty seconds of a two-chord figure with guitar, keyboards, and drums before the vocals start. Vintage soul is considered to be the main influence on this song, not least the singing of Otis Redding, Percy Sledge, and, in particular, Wilson Pickett on his early hit 'It's Too Late'. Less than three minutes in, it reaches a crescendo with Page's impassioned solo that extends over the next minute of the song, before Plant returns for a final verse and ad-libbing up to the end. The general effect is like an updated version of 'You Shook Me', but with the synth adding a more contemporary gloss—one which some might contend makes it sound a little dated.

Its working title, 'The Blot', was given to the mono mix that appeared in 2015 on the deluxe edition.

It was never performed live by the group on stage, but became part of the set list of the group formed by the drummer's son, Jason Bonham's Led Zeppelin Experience, on their worldwide 2011 tour.

10

Coda

UK: released 22 November 1982, Swan Song, No. 4 (2015 reissue, No. 9)
US: released 19 November 1982, Swan Song, No. 6
Current edition: Swan Song CD
Personnel: Robert Plant—lead vocals, harmonica
Jimmy Page—electric and acoustic guitars, Gizmotron
John Paul Jones—bass guitar, piano, keyboards
John Bonham—drums, percussion
Recorded at various studios, 1970–78, plus overdubs 1982, Polar Studios, Stockholm, November–December 1978
Produced by Jimmy Page

In musical terms, a coda is the name given to a passage that concludes a musical piece after the main part of the work. It was a fitting title for the ninth and last album of studio material, comprising unused tracks from various sessions recorded throughout their twelve-year career, released two years after the group had disbanded following the death of Bonham.

Page explained that part of the reason for the album's release was the large amount of bootlegs in circulation, and that as there was so much interest, they might as well make it legitimately available. It was also released to honour contractual commitments to Atlantic who were owed one more album under the terms of their contract, and to cover tax demands on previous monies earned. It entered the album charts on both sides of the Atlantic comfortably in the Top 10, but after initial sales to the group's fan base, interest soon waned. In Britain, London's Oxford Street was a fertile hunting ground for bargain bin stocks before long.

Side one contains four tracks, two being live recordings from 1970 later doctored in the studio, and two studio cuts from the early or mid-70s, while side two consists of three outtakes from, and an unused drum track from 1976.

The album cover was once again the work of the Hipgnosis group, their fifth for Led Zeppelin and their last major project before they disbanded in 1983. The letters CODA are taken from an alphabet typeface design, Neon, designed in 1978.

A 1993 CD edition includes four additional tracks from the box sets issued in 1990 and 1993 (see below, p. 118), the previously unreleased 'Travelling Riverside Blues', 'White Summer/Black Mountain Side', and 'Hey, Hey, What Can I Do', from the first, and 'Baby Come on Home' from the second.

A remastered version of *Coda* was released in July 2015 in six formats: a standard CD edition, a deluxe three-CD edition, a standard LP version, a deluxe three-LP version, a super deluxe three-CD plus three-LP version with a hardback book, and as high-resolution 96k/24-bit digital downloads. The deluxe and super deluxe editions feature bonus material containing alternative takes and retitled or previously unreleased songs: 'If It Keeps On Raining' (a rough mix of 'When the Levee Breaks'), 'Sugar Mama', 'Four Hands', 'St Tristan's Sword', and 'Desire' (a rough mix of 'The Wanton Song'). The reissue included an inverted colour version of the original album's artwork as its bonus disc's cover.

Tracks

1. 'We're Gonna Groove' (James Bethea, Ben E. King) 2.37

Originally written and recorded as a single in 1960 under the title 'Groovin'', by Ben E. King and his songwriting partner James Bethea, it was covered four years later by Manfred Mann as 'We're Gonna Groove', and Led Zeppelin featured it as the opening number during their 1970 UK and European tours. They had intended to include it on their second album, but it was excluded presumably for reasons of space.

According to the accompanying credits, their version was recorded at Morgan Studios, London, on 25 June 1969, but later research proved that it was from a Royal Albert Hall concert on 9 January 1970, with audience noise and the original guitar part removed and additional guitar parts overdubbed. The January 1970 concert performance with the original guitar part can be heard on the two-DVD set, *Led Zeppelin*, issued in 2003, on which the first disc features material from the 1970 concert.

For the British, European, and American dates during the first four months of 1970, this song always opened their set, to be dropped after that and replaced by 'Immigrant Song'. Page and Plant revived it to use in part in the 'Calling to You/Whole Lotta Love' medleys on their 1995–96 world tour, and Plant performed it in full on his dates with Priory of Brion in 1999–2000.

2. 'Poor Tom' (Page, Plant) 3.02

A folksy, jug band-style number written in 1970 by Page and Plant while they were staying at Bron-Yr-Aur, it was recorded at Olympic Studios on 5 June that year and considered for inclusion on *Led Zeppelin III*. The lyrics tell of 'Poor Tom, seventh son, always knew what's goin' on'. Tradition has it that a seventh son has special powers, such as being psychic, having the ability to tell fortunes, and, in this case, realising that his wife is cheating on him, something for which she pays with a bullet in her head.

Bonham opens the song with a soft shuffling beat on the snare, while Page's acoustic guitar is tuned to an open-C6 chord (C-A-C-G-C-E) and played in the style of John Renbourn and Bert Jansch. There are similarities with Robert Wilkins's 'Prodigal Son', as recorded by The Rolling Stones, and the riff is reminiscent of John Fahey's 1963 guitar instrumental 'Sunflower River Blues'. Plant adds harmonica towards the end of the song. They never performed it live on stage.

3. 'I Can't Quit You Baby' (Willie Dixon) 4.18

This was a rather strange choice for the record, as it does not differ markedly from the version that appeared on the group's debut album (see p. 27). This recording from the 9 January 1970 show is about twenty seconds shorter, Page's guitar solo is a little cleaner, and the ending is a more dramatic tempest of feedback, followed by a less restrained storm on the drums. The original credits noted it as a taped on a rehearsal at the Royal Albert Hall for the concert at which 'We're Gonna Groove' above was played. Again, the 2003 DVD set suggests that this also comes from the concert, as both sound almost identical, apart from being a different mix and once more with all crowd noise removed.

4. 'Walter's Walk' (Page, Plant) 4.31

A frantic, dirty, and uncomplicated sound built around Page's guitar riffs as Plant sings a song of frustrated love with a refrain of 'I'm walkin' the floor over you' and Bonham's drums at full throttle almost from start to fade, this began life as a backing track laid down at Stargroves in May 1972 during sessions for *Houses of the Holy*. It seems to have remained thus for almost ten years, until Plant added a vocal at Page's news Sol Studios at Cookham.

It was never performed live in full. Parts of the riff were included in 'Dazed and Confused' during the tours of 1972 and 1973, as the twenty-five-minute version on the three-CD *How the West was Won* notes, as well as also being used in 'Hots On for Nowhere', recorded during the sessions for *Presence* in 1975.

5. 'Ozone Baby' (Page, Plant) 3.36

This was the first of three tracks recorded in November 1978 at Polar Studios during sessions for *In Through the Out Door* but not included on the album, mainly for reasons of space; these three tracks were briefly considered the following year for an EP (see under 'Wearing and Tearing', p. 112). None of them contained anything in the way of a deep lyric, with no veiled allusions to troubled group member chemistry or even a whiff of Tolkienesque-inspired visions or references to Norse legends. Each one sounded more like a return to the group famed for the by-now timeless 'Communication Breakdown' and 'Whole Lotta Love' than anything that appeared on the album. In just three and a half minutes, they deliver a punch number that starts off with a twangy guitar-bass-drums riff and continues in the same vein with Plant singing in the refrain 'Ooh-ooh, it's my own true love', with a few stops and restarts towards the end. It was ample proof that, like The Rolling Stones and The Who, they could focus their creative talents delivering radio-friendly anthems without selling out to the lowest common denominator.

None of these three songs ever made it to the group's stage show, although parts of 'Ozone Baby' were used in the arrangements for 'Dazed and Confused' on the 1975 American tour.

6. 'Darlene' (Bonham, Jones, Page, Plant) 5.06

The second Polar Studios song that might have been part of their bid for a hit 45 is almost a sprightly rock 'n' roll song, and the only one from their final sessions jointly credited to all four members. Moreover, it is the only song the group wrote and recorded that took its title from a girl's name, even if on the first few listens it sounds as if Plant is singing about 'Double E'. Page goes down the rockabilly path on guitar, while Jones's barrelhouse piano adds to the good-time atmosphere.

7. 'Bonzo's Montreux' (Bonham) 4.22

A drum solo by Bonham, recorded in September 1976 at Mountain Studios, Montreux, Switzerland, was only the second number they recorded as a showcase for the instrument, the first being 'Moby Dick'. Page added synthesiser and studio effects afterwards. It was also included on both of the band's boxed sets, released in the early 1990s, as a medley with 'Moby Dick' on the first boxed set in 1990 and as an individual track on the second in 1993. Although the version of *Coda* included on *The Complete Studio Recordings* boxed set featured the new songs that were released on the boxed set series, the 'Moby Dick/Bonzo's Montreux' medley on the first boxed set in 1990 was omitted.

8. 'Wearing and Tearing' (Page, Plant) 5.27

One of the three songs from the last album session, it undoubtedly reflects the two writers' enthusiasm for and interest in punk rock, especially The Damned, whom they had been to see live together in London. Page had been full of praise for their debut album, said that new wave was the most important thing to happen in music since Jimi Hendrix had arrived in London, and had called a couple of Sex Pistols' tracks 'really great', although he had less time for their negative outlook. His admiration for the new breed was not reciprocated, least of all by The Clash, one of whom said he only needed to see a Led Zeppelin album sleeve in order to throw up.

It is one of the few Zeppelin tunes that sustains a seriously fast tempo throughout, an exhilarating rock workout with one or two brief stops and starts along the way. To music critics, it was more than adequate evidence that they could compete with the contemporary punk bands that were dismissing them—that it was 'proof that when it came to energy and aggression, punk rockers had nothing on the Zep ... pure China-shop bull charge with Page slashing out chords and tearing through high-speed riffs'.[1]

Shortly before the group appeared at Knebworth in August 1979, there was speculation that this number would break new ground for the group in being released as a single in Britain. Plant was particularly enthusiastic, commenting that 'we did that song with the intention of saying, "OK, we're dinosaurs and boring old farts, try a little bit of this"'. Page, who had until then been noted for his resistance to issuing Led Zeppelin 45s in their home country, wanted it as the lead track on an EP also containing 'Ozone Baby' and 'Darlene'.[2] Significantly, Black Sabbath and a couple of Deep Purple offshoots, Rainbow and Whitesnake, each had minor chart success with singles and EPs during the summer of 1978, and two of them even promoted them with studio appearances on BBC TV's *Top of the Pops*. Maybe Led Zeppelin felt inspired to consider the challenge (as did Pink Floyd, another group who for years refused to issue singles in Britain and then landed 'Another Brick in the Wall Part II' at No. 1 for Christmas 1979). It was also rumoured that they might release the record under another name so that it would not be prejudged simply because it was regarded as desperately uncool by some of the more hip rock press. Whether they would have risked it going into record shops with an alias and watching it disappear into bargain bins for lack of interest is another matter entirely. Perhaps through lack of time, nothing came of the plan.

Copies of a 45 rpm single with 'Wearing and Tearing' on the A-side and 'Darlene' on the flip are known, although there is speculation this could be either a promo, a planned and then cancelled release, or even a bootleg. It was allocated a catalogue number of SSK 19421, which (unlike the number for the cancelled 'Whole Lotta Love' ten years earlier) was not reallocated to a subsequent Swan Song release, suggesting that it may have had the full sanction of group and management without ever coming to fruition.

Bonus Tracks

The 1993 CD edition includes four additional tracks from the box sets issued in 1990 and 1993 (see below, p. 118): 'Travelling Riverside Blues', 'White Summer/Black Mountain Side', and 'Hey, Hey, What Can I Do', from the first, and 'Baby Come on Home' from the second.

'Travelling Riverside Blues' (Robert Johnson, Page, Plant) 5.08

Recorded on a BBC session on 24 June 1969, this five-minute blues workout includes Page playing twelve-string acoustic slide guitar and later on a solo on six-string electric, with Jones and Bonham supplying an unobtrusive rhythm section. The lyrics are based largely on Johnson's original, recorded some thirty years earlier, with sufficient alterations from Page and Plant to give themselves a co-writing credits. Some of this was the ad-libbing, including 'squeeze my lemon' and 'why don't you come into my kitchen' metaphors, frequently used by Johnson himself in his lyrics and thus giving the lie to politically correct assertions during the 1970s that Led Zeppelin were foremost among hard rock groups in being responsible for the craze for crude or misogynistic lyrics.

A one-track promo CD single was issued for American radio stations in 1990.

'White Summer/Black Mountain Side' (Page) 8.01

Recorded live on 27 June 1969 at the Playhouse Theatre, London, for a pilot of BBC Radio 1's new *In Concert* series, its first release was on the *Led Zeppelin Boxed Set.* A lengthy instrumental incorporating Indian and Arabic musical influences, 'White Summer' was credited to Page but based on the Irish folk song 'She Moved Through the Fair', in particular an adaptation by Davy Graham, and Page initially recorded a four-minute version while he was a member of The Yardbirds on their final album *Little Games*, released in 1967 only in America. Page also based the first section of 'Over the Hills and Far Away' on the theme.

The group—or rather Page sitting on a stool with his Danelectro guitar, with occasional drum fills from Bonham—often performed it with the much shorter 'Black Mountain Side' (see p. 25) being integrated into the middle, during the tours of 1969 and 1970, reviving it for the 1977 American dates and their last shows in 1979 and 1980. Page also played it on a rare solo TV appearance in April 1970 as a guest on the Julie Felix BBC series *Once More with Felix*. In his post-Led Zeppelin days, he also played it when touring with The Firm, and again while promoting his 1988 solo album *Outrider*.

'Hey, Hey, What Can I Do' (Bonham, Jones, Page, Plant) 3.52

Recorded at Island Studios during sessions for the third album, this was unique in the group's back catalogue as their only non-album B-side, being coupled with 'Immigrant Song' when it was issued as a 45 throughout most of the world. In their home country, it was only available on the budget price (99p, compared to the average full-price album which then sold at £2.25–£2.50) on Atlantic Records various artists compilation album *The New Age of Atlantic*, released in November 1972, also featuring material by Yes, Buffalo Springfield, Gordon Haskell, John Prine, and Loudon Wainwright III among others, and charting at No. 25. Its first CD appearance was in September 1990 on the four-CD *Led Zeppelin Boxed Set* collection.

Like many of the other songs written at Bron-Yr-Aur, it is a relaxed, folk-meets-country song, one of the few they ever recorded that features a recognisable chorus, on which Page and Bonham join in with backing vocals. Whether it is a paean to unrequited love and romance or to a prostitute with its references to a 'street corner girl' is up to the listener. Page and Jones play acoustic six-string and twelve-string guitars, to which Page adds zither and Jones bass guitar and mandolin. With its general acoustic feel, it is not far removed from some of the more folk-rock tunes Rod Stewart was recording at the time on his first solo albums. For the most part, Plant sings in a lower register, only rising to semi-scream mode on the last line of the choruses ('I said I got a little woman and she won't be true') and for the constant repetition of the title towards the end, with minor improvised variations on same, which turns into a magnificent crescendo of the others singing the title over and over again while his ad-libs morph into a vast sea of echo. Just when it sounds like it ought to fade out, it comes to an endearingly ragged spontaneous end with the rhythm section downing tools while the mandolin continues a little longer, leaving the acoustic guitar to wander off at a tangent elsewhere for the last few seconds.

There was speculation that the group or Grant considered releasing it as a stand-alone A-side single in Britain. Deep Purple, Free, Black Sabbath, and Ten Years After all enjoyed major singles chart success in 1970, and Led Zeppelin would have been in good company had they done so as well.

The group never played it live, but Page and Plant featured it regularly on their 1995–96 tour, Page with The Black Crowes while touring with them in concert in 1999, and Plant sometimes with Strange Sensation when touring in 2002. Several Plant and Page performances available on YouTube at the time of writing have the song in a higher key than the recorded version ('A' as opposed to 'G'), with Page playing rhythm on the twelve-string part of a double-neck acoustic guitar. When the camera cuts away from Page, Plant, and the group on stage to shots of the audience, singing along, dancing, and rhythmically raising an arm in the air, it becomes clear that this was one of the group's most infectious songs that could certainly have landed them major British singles chart success if only they and the management had not set themselves so firmly against the idea. It was later covered by Hootie & the Blowfish.

'Baby Come on Home' (Bert Berns, Page, Plant) 4.30

Recorded during sessions for the first album, and rumoured to have been briefly considered as a single early in 1970, this was missing, presumed lost, until renovations at Olympic Studios in 1991, when a master reel marked 'Yardbirds, October 10, 1968' was found in a refuse bin and then remixed by producer Mike Fraser, who was working on an album by Page and David Coverdale at the time. Originally called 'Tribute to Bert Berns', in honour of the American songwriter and producer who had died of heart failure the previous year, it is a rock ballad in waltz time reminiscent of Berns's style—hence the joint writer's credit—and also in structure quite similar to the much-covered soul classic 'Stay With Me Baby'.

Page's guitar is played through a Leslie speaker, while Jones contributes piano and Hammond organ. It is that rarity among Zeppelin tracks, a song with powerful backing vocals, presumably the work of Page and Jones and maybe Bonham as well.

The 2015 Deluxe Three-CD Edition

'If It Keeps On Raining' (Bonham, Jones, Memphis Minnie, Page, Plant) 4.11

This was the group's first version of 'When the Levee Breaks', recorded in December 1970, possibly at Headley Grange but more likely at Island Studios, during initial sessions for the fourth album. Being dissatisfied with the result, they abandoned it for a few months and started afresh five months later. The second version lasted seven minutes, but this earlier take is nearly three minutes shorter. It features a much less lengthy intro and no harmonica. The drums are more of a bluesy shuffle than the thunderous stomp, and it fades out at the end.

'Sugar Mama (Mix)' (Page, Plant) 2.50

Recorded in October 1968, this is a loosely customized version of 'Sugar Mama', as recorded by Yank Rachell and then by Tampa Red around 1934, then three years later by Sonny Boy Williamson, who is generally thought to have been the writer. Fleetwood Mac recorded their own version at around the same time as Led Zeppelin. This completely alters the laid-back bluesy tempo of the others, and with the stabbing guitar chords on the intro and the more up-tempo, pop meets rock 'n' roll groove. If it had not been for Plant's unmistakable wailing vocal out front, it could almost have passed for an early Kinks tune. Page plays rhythm, lead, and slide guitars, while Jones can be heard on Hammond organ and bass pedals as well as bass guitar. Had it appeared on the first album, like 'Baby Come on Home' (which was taped at the same session), it might have sounded rather out of character alongside the longer, slower blues tracks.

'Four Hands' ('Four Sticks') 4.43

A re-recording of the number from the fourth album, made by Page and Plant in 1972, during their trip to India, this one being an instrumental version featuring sitars and tabla drums.

'Friends' (Page, Plant) 4.25

A re-recording of the song from the third album, made with the Bombay Symphony Orchestra at the same time as the previous track, although this is not an instrumental. Page's acoustic guitar comes in after forty seconds of the drone of the Indian instruments as does the tabla, with Plant's vocals joining in another forty seconds after that. If the original only hinted at the Eastern influences at play, this version embraces them wholeheartedly.

'St Tristan's Sword' (Page) 5.40

An instrumental recorded at the sessions for the third album, this features a funky guitar riff with Jones's bass guitar more prominent than usual, and Bonham unleashing fireworks as ever on the drums. Page commented that it was the kind of tune they would play spontaneously on stage during another number, 'veering off into something' and then reverting to the main number. It was a case of suddenly hitting on a riff out of the blue, trying it and making a mental note of anything that worked particularly well, to commit to tape afterwards. There was never a St Tristan, but the legend of Tristan, the Arthurian knight, and his love for the Irish Princess Iseult is said to have inspired the love story of Lancelot and Guinevere. Plant's fascination with ancient legends was presumably the source for the title.

'Desire' (Page, Plant) 4.08

A rough mix of the 'Wanton Song' that, apart from differences in sound quality (sounding more distorted), is very similar to the released version. The main difference is in the more basic guitar work, this one lacking the overdubs, especially the solo played through a Leslie speaker on the finished product.

'Everybody Makes it Through' (Jones, Page, Plant) 8.31

A rough mix of 'In the Light', about fifteen seconds shorter than the original on *Physical Graffiti*. This contains the alternate lyrics, beginning 'Sunshine brings laughter', and has an additional organ riff playing a descending four-note sequence over part of the drone in the early part of the song just before the vocals enter on the first verse.

11

Compilation and Live Albums

Led Zeppelin Boxed Set

UK: released 23 October 1990, Atlantic, No. 48
US: released 23 October 1990, Atlantic, No. 18

This contains fifty-four tracks from the group's studio albums on four CDs, all previously released apart from 'Travelling Riverside Blues', 'Hey, Hey, What Can I Do', 'White Summer/Black Mountain Side' (see p. 113), and 'Moby Dick/Bonzo's Montreux', a previously unreleased mix, five minutes long, of both tracks.

Led Zeppelin Boxed Set 2

UK: released 19 March 1993, Atlantic, No. 56
US: released 19 March 1993, Atlantic, No. 87
Produced by Jimmy Page

This contains the remaining thirty-two tracks from the group's studio albums not included on the earlier set, on two CDs, all previously released apart from 'Baby Come On Home' (see p. 115).

The Complete Studio Recordings

UK: released 24 September 1993, Atlantic
US: released 24 September 1993, Atlantic
Produced by Jimmy Page

This contains all nine original studio albums digitally remastered, plus an expanded version of *Coda*, on ten CDs. It was withdrawn four years later and replaced by the *Definitive Collection* Mini LP Replica CD boxed set, released by Atlantic/Rhino Entertainment on 4 November 2008.

Four bonus tracks were added to the *Coda* deluxe reissue, 'Baby Come On Home', which had appeared on *Led Zeppelin Boxed Set 2*, plus some of the previously unreleased tracks that had surfaced on the 1990 boxed set, namely 'Travelling Riverside Blues', 'White Summer/Black Mountain Side', and 'Hey, Hey, What Can I Do'. All three tracks were released on a small quantity of promotional CD EPs at the same time as the boxed set, as were a few one-track promos. The expanded version of *Coda* included in the boxed set was made available to digital stores in 2007 with the digital release of the entire Led Zeppelin catalogue, with 'Travelling Riverside Blues' omitted as it was already available on *BBC Sessions*.

The Song Remains the Same

UK: released 22 October 1976, Swan Song, No. 1 for one week (2007 reissue, No. 73)
US: released 22 October 1976, Swan Song, No. 2
Produced by Jimmy Page

'Rock and Roll', 'Celebration Day', 'The Song Remains the Same', 'The Rain Song', 'Dazed and Confused', ''No Quarter', 'Stairway to Heaven', 'Moby Dick', and 'Whole Lotta Love'.

The reissue added 'Black Dog' (with 'Bring It On Home' intro), 'Over the Hills and Far Away', 'Misty Mountain Hop', 'Since I've Been Lovin' You', 'The Ocean', and 'Heartbreaker'. All recorded 27–29 July 1973, Madison Square Garden, New York City

How the West was Won

UK: released 27 May 2003, Atlantic, No. 5
US: released 27 May 2003, Atlantic, No. 1 for one week
Produced by Jimmy Page

'LA Drone', 'Immigrant Song', 'Heartbreaker', 'Black Dog', 'Over the Hills and Far Away', 'Since I've Been Loving You', 'Stairway to Heaven', 'Going to California', 'That's the Way', 'Bron-Yr-Aur Stomp', 'Dazed and Confused', 'What Is and What Should Never Be', 'Dancing Days', 'Moby Dick', 'Whole

Lotta Love', 'Rock and Roll', 'The Ocean', 'Bring it on Home', recorded at the LA Forum, 25 June 1972, and Long Beach Arena, two days later. Two numbers last over twenty minutes each and integrate part of additional tracks. 'Dazed and Confused' (25.25) contains some of 'Walter's Walk' and 'The Crunge', while 'Whole Lotta Love' (23.08) has a medley including 'Boogie Chillun', 'Let's Have a Party', 'Hello Mary Lou', and 'Going Down Slow'.

Celebration Day

UK: released 19 November 2012, Atlantic, No. 4
US: released 19 November 2012, Atlantic, No. 9
Produced by Jimmy Page

'Good Times Bad Times', 'Ramble On', 'Black Dog', 'In My Time Of Dying', 'For Your Life', 'Trampled Under Foot', 'Nobody's Fault but Mine', 'No Quarter', 'Since I've Been Loving You', 'Dazed and Confused', 'Stairway to Heaven', 'The Song Remains the Same', 'Misty Mountain Hop', 'Kashmir', 'Whole Lotta Love', and 'Rock and Roll', recorded at the O2 Arena, London, 10 December 2007, released in a standard edition consisting of one DVD or Blu-ray plus two soundtrack CDs, with a triple vinyl following a few weeks later.

BBC Sessions

UK: released 17 November 1997, Atlantic, No. 23 (2016 reissue, No. 3)
US: released 18 November 1997, Atlantic, No. 12 (2016 reissue, No. 21)
Album produced by Jimmy Page (individual sessions originally produced by Bernie Andrews, Jeff Griffin, Paul Williams, John Walters)

'You Shook Me', 'I Can't Quit You Baby', 'Communication Breakdown', Dazed and Confused', 'The Girl I Love She Got Long Black Wavy Hair', 'What Is and What Should Never Be', 'Communication Breakdown', 'Travelling Riverside Blues', 'Whole Lotta Love', 'Somethin' Else', 'Communication Breakdown', 'I Can't Quit You Baby', 'You Shook Me', 'How Many More Times', 'Immigrant Song', 'Heartbreaker', 'Since I've Been Loving You', 'Black Dog', 'Dazed and Confused', 'Stairway to Heaven', Going to California', That's the Way', 'Whole Lotta Love (Medley)', and 'Thank You'. All songs up to 'How Many More Times' are taken from four different 1969 BBC sessions, and the rest comprise most of a live concert recorded at the Paris Theatre, London, 1 April 1971. 'Whole Lotta Love (Medley)' includes 'Boogie Chillun'/Fixin' To Die/

That's Alright Mama/A Mess of Blues'. Only three of the songs, the two below and 'Travelling Riverside Blues' (see p. 113), did not also appear on their first four studio albums.

'The Girl I Love She Got Long Black Wavy Hair' (Bonham, Jones, Page, Plant, John Estes) 3.00

Adapted from a song of the same title first recorded by Sleepy John Estes in 1929, it was recorded by the group at the end of their mini-tour of Britain on 16 June 1969 for a BBC Radio 1 session, and broadcast six days later on *Chris Grant's Tasty Pop Sundae* show. This was probably the only performance of the number they ever gave, or at least recorded. The distinctive twelve-bar blues riff played by Page would become the basis for 'Moby Dick', the showcase for Bonham's drumming on their second album which they were also working on at the time.

'Somethin' Else' (Bob Cochran, Sharon Sheeley) 2.06

This fast, frantic, and joyous retread of the song that in 1959 gave the pioneering rock 'n' roller Eddie Cochran his second British hit (the co-writers being his girlfriend and his elder brother), and which would be his only British top ten entry during his lifetime, was a frequent staple of the group's gigs in the early days. They generally played it back-to-back with his other classic 'C'mon Everybody', as can be seen and heard on the 9 January 1970 Royal Albert Hall DVD recording. For once there is no lead break, and the instrumental honours go instead to Jones with a spirited boogie solo on piano. Coincidentally, both songs were successfully revived in 1979 as singles by The Sex Pistols.

The Complete BBC Sessions

UK: released 16 September 2016, Atlantic, No. 3
US: released 16 September 2016, Atlantic, No. 21
Album produced by Jimmy Page (individual sessions originally produced by Bernie Andrews, Jeff Griffin, Paul Williams, John Walters)

An expanded reissue of the previous set, with a third CD comprising 'Communication Breakdown', 'What Is and What Should Never Be', 'Dazed and Confused', 'White Summer', 'What Is and What Should Never Be', 'Communication Breakdown', 'I Can't Quit You Baby', 'You Shook Me', and 'Sunshine Woman', the first four and last three tracks being sessions from

1969, the other two from the concert at the Paris Theatre, London, 1 April 1971. 'White Summer' had previously been released in 1990 on the boxed set, the expanded 1993 reissue of *Coda*, and the 2008 boxed set. A long-lost three-song session, from March 1969, believed to have been erased from master tapes and sourced from a lo-fi recording made from an AM radio by a listener at home (obviously in mono), includes two songs that appeared on the first studio album and one previously unreleased one as below.

'Sunshine Woman' (Bonham, Willie Dixon, Robert Johnson, Jones, Page, Plant) 3.06

A funky, spontaneous twelve-bar blues with Bonham's drums on the full attack, Page unleashing a sonic extravaganza on guitar, Plant and his harmonica in full cry, and Jones presumably giving his all on the piano. Page said it had basically all been improvised on the spur of the moment: 'It was pretty brave, bearing in mind the circumstances. We played it as if we were in rehearsals, starting it around the riff and then working it out. It shows that we were evolving pretty quickly'. As it borrowed to some extent on songs from two of the original blues masters, six joint writers were credited.[1] The BBC sessions that Led Zeppelin recorded in their early days were very important in their development as a group. Jones said that few other acts were making a practice of the kind of improvising they were at the time and the Corporation allowed them full scope to go ahead on the radio, particularly on the later *In Concert* recordings: 'This was in the days of restricted needle time so we were determined to make the best of every BBC radio opportunity'.[2]

Endnotes

* Online sources; for full details and URL see Bibliography

Introduction

1. Robinson, L., 'Stairway to Excess', *Vanity Fair,* 18 February 2014.

Chapter 1

1. Long, A., 'Get the Led Out…'*.
2. Tobler, J., & Grundy, S., *The Guitar Greats* (BBC, 1983), pp. 101-102.
3. Yorke, R., *Led Zeppelin: From Early Days to Page and Plant* (Virgin, 1999), p. 72.
4. Wall, M., *When Giants Walked the Earth: A Biography of Led Zeppelin* (Griffin, 2010), p. 71.
5. Tolinski, B., 'Led Vault…'*.
6. Wall, M., *op. cit.*, p. 67.
7. *Ibid.*, p. 58.
8. Harper, C., *Dazzling Stranger: Bert Jansch and the British Folk and Blues Revival* (Bloomsbury, 2006), p. 5.
9. Tobler, J., & Grundy, S., *op. cit.*, p. 102.
10. Schulps, D., 'Interview with Jimmy Page', *Guitar World*, January 1993.

Chapter 2

1. Rosen, S., 'Interview with Jimmy Page', *Guitar Player*, July 1977.
2. Tobler, J., & Grundy, S., *The Guitar Greats* (BBC, 1983), p. 103.
3. Myers, M., 'The Making of Led Zeppelin's "Whole Lotta Love"', *Wall Street Journal*, 29 May 2014.
4. Wall, M., *When Giants Walked the Earth: A Biography of Led Zeppelin* (Griffin, 2010), p. 155.
5. Young, C. M., 'Robert Plant's manic persona', *Musician*, June 1990.
6. Hann, M., 'Yes, Led Zeppelin took from other people's records—but then they transformed them', *The Guardian*, 12 April 2016.

7. Wall, M., *op. cit.*, p. 158.
8. Tobler & Grundy, *op. cit.*, p. 103.
9. Coleman, N., 'Why Led Zeppelin's "Whole Lotta Love" will always be *Top of the Pops, The Independent*, 30 April 1998.
10. Slash names his Top 12 Guitarists*.
11. Selby, J., 'Led Zeppelin guitarist Jimmy Page: '"Olympics with Leona Lewis is my greatest achievement"', *The Independent*, 26 November 2014.
12. Tobler, J., & Grundy, S., *op. cit.*, p. 105.
13. Davis, S., *Hammer of the Gods: Led Zeppelin unauthorised* (Pan, 2008), p. 96.

Chapter 3

1. Bangs, L., 'Led Zeppelin III', review, *Rolling Stone*, 26 November 1970.
2. Rogers, J., 'A life in music: Robert Plant on Led Zeppelin, Alison Krauss and his endless wanderlust', *The Guardian*, 2 November 2016.
3. Tobler, J., & Grundy, S., *The Guitar Greats* (BBC, 1983), p. 104.
4. Schulps, D., Interview with Jimmy Page, *Guitar World*, January 1993.
5. Wall, M., *When Giants Walked the Earth: A Biography of Led Zeppelin* (Griffin, 2010), p. 201.

Chapter 4

1. Jackson, J., 'Jimmy Page on *Led Zeppelin IV*, the band's peak and their reunion', *The Times*, 8 January 2010.
2. Schulps, D., Interview with Jimmy Page, *Guitar World*, January 1993.
3. Tobler, J., & Grundy, S., *The Guitar Greats* (BBC, 1983), p. 105.
4. Ramirez, A. J., 'All that Glitters: Led Zeppelin—"The Battle of Evermore"', *Pop Matters,* 31 October 2011.
5. Wall, M., *When Giants Walked the Earth: A Biography of Led Zeppelin* (Griffin, 2010), p. 253.
6. Good Times...Bad Times', *Uncut*, 57, May 2005.
7. Jackson, J., 'Good times, bad times, you know I've had my share', *The Times*, 8 January 2010.
8 Wall, M., *op. cit.*, p. 255.
9. Crowe, C., Interview with Jimmy Page, *Rolling Stone*, 13 March 1975.
10. Wall, M., *op. cit.*, p. 255.
11. Considine, J. D., 'Led Zeppelin', *Rolling Stone,* 26 September 1990.
12. *Los Angeles Times*, 6 December 1988.
13. Hann, M., '"Stairway to Heaven": The Story of a Song and its Legacy', *The Guardian*, 22 October 2014.
14. Carroll, R., 'Led Zeppelin fend off claim of "Stairway to Heaven" plagiarism', *The Guardian*, 24 June 2016.
15. *Billboard*, 18 June 2016.
16. Wall, M., *op. cit.*, p. 257.
17. Hann, M., *op. cit.*
18. Alan Freeman obituary, *The Times*, 29 November 2006.
19. 'Best album of all time', *The Times*, 18 December 1993.
20. Wall, M., *op. cit.*, pp. 40, 254.

Chapter 5

Lewis, D., *Led Zeppelin: From a Whisper to a Scream: Complete Guide to Their Music* (Omnibus, 2012), p. 61.

Chapter 7

1. Hann, M., 'Yes, Led Zeppelin took from other people's records—but then they transformed them', *The Guardian*, 12 April 2016.
2. Wall, M., *When Giants Walked the Earth: A Biography of Led Zeppelin* (Griffin, 2010), pp. 68-69.
3. Hann, M., 'Jimmy Page on Led Zeppelin's "Kashmir": "You need time to catch your breath after"', *The Guardian*, 27 February 2015.
4. Wall, M., *op. cit.*, p. 341.
5. Tobler, J., & Grundy, S., *The Guitar Greats* (BBC, 1983), pp. 105-106.
6. Jimmy Page tells the story of "Kashmir"'. Open Culture*.
7. Simpson, D., 'Noddy Holder: "People think I live in a cave all year and come out in December, shouting 'It's Chriiisstmaaasss!'"', *The Guardian*, 26 November 2015.
8. Paphides, P., 'Old boys rock heaven and hell for the mothership of all reunions', *The Times*, 11 December 2007.
9. Tobler, J., & Grundy, S., *op. cit.*, p. 106.
10. Tolinski, B., *Light and Shade: Conversations with Jimmy Page* (Crown, 2012), p. 56.
11. Alexander, P., 'Up Close & Personal', *Mojo*, February 2010.
12. Wall, M., *op. cit.*, p. 342.

Chapter 8

1. Schulps, D., Interview with Jimmy Page.
2. Fricke, D., 'Robert Plant on the Led Zeppelin Rehearsals: The Band Has "Done It. It's There"', *Rolling Stone*, 13 December 2007.
3. Rogers, J., 'A life in music: Robert Plant on Led Zeppelin, Alison Krauss and his endless wanderlust', *The Guardian*, 2 November 2016.
4. Schulps, D., Interview with Jimmy Page, *Guitar World*, January 1993.
5. Tobler, J., & Grundy, S., *The Guitar Greats* (BBC, 1983), p. 106.
6. Schulps, D., Interview with Jimmy Page, *Guitar World*, January 1993.
7. Wall, M., *When Giants Walked the Earth: A Biography of Led Zeppelin* (Griffin, 2010), p. 365.

Chapter 9

1. Snow, M., 'Apocalypse Then', *Q Magazine*, December 1990.
2. Hann, M., 'Jimmy Page: "Robert and I went to see the Damned. He'd probably run a mile from that now"' (interview), *The Guardian*, 24 July 2015.
3. Williamson, N., *The Rough Guide to Led Zeppelin* (Rough Guides, 2007), p. 238.
4. Lewis, D., *Led Zeppelin: From a Whisper to a Scream: Complete Guide to Their Music* (Amsco, 2013), p. 93.

5. Davis, S., *Hammer of the Gods: Led Zeppelin unauthorised* (Pan, 2008), p. 284.
6. All Music Guide review, 'In Through the Out Door'*.
7. Wall, M., *When Giants Walked the Earth: A Biography of Led Zeppelin* (Griffin, 2010), p. 415.
8. Snow, M., *op. cit.*
9. Brad Tolinski, B., and Benedetto, G. Di, Light and Shade*.

Chapter 10

1. Drozdowski, T., 'Celebration Day*: Jimmy Page's Top 10 Guitar Moments'*.
2. Davis, S., *Hammer of the Gods: Led Zeppelin unauthorised* (Pan, 2008), p. 285.

Chapter 11

1. Alexander, P., 'Jimmy Page reveals all about Led Zeppelin's new *Complete BBC Sessions* and its "lost" tracks', *Mojo*, October 2016.
2. Wall, M., *When Giants Walked the Earth: A Biography of Led Zeppelin* (Griffin, 2010), p. 135.

Bibliography

Books

Davis, S., *Hammer of the Gods: Led Zeppelin unauthorised* (Pan, 2008)
Harper, C., *Dazzling Stranger: Bert Jansch and the British Folk and Blues Revival* (Bloomsbury, 2006)
Hoskyns, B., *Trampled Under Foot: The Power and Excess of Led Zeppelin* (Faber, 2012)
Lewis, D., *Led Zeppelin: A Celebration* (Omnibus, 2003); *Led Zeppelin: From a Whisper to a Scream: Complete Guide to Their Music* (Omnibus, 2012)
Popoff, M., *Led Zeppelin: All the Albums, All the Songs* (Voyageur, 2017)
Rees, P., *Robert Plant: A Life* (HarperCollins, 2013)
Shadwick, K., *Led Zeppelin: The Story of a Band and Their Music 1968-1980* (Backbeat, 2005)
Tobler, J., & Grundy, S., *The Guitar Greats* (BBC, 1983)
Tolinski, B., *Light and Shade: Conversations with Jimmy Page* (Crown, 2012)
Wall, M., *When Giants Walked the Earth: A Biography of Led Zeppelin* (Griffin, 2010)
Welch, C., *Led Zeppelin: The stories behind every Led Zeppelin song* (Carlton, 2009)
Williamson, N., *The Rough Guide to Led Zeppelin* (Rough Guides, 2007)
Yorke, R., *Led Zeppelin: From Early Days to Page and Plant* (Virgin, 1999)

Journals and Newspapers

Billboard: 18 June 2016
Guardian: 22 October 2014, 27 February 2015, 24 July 2015, 26 November 2015, 12 April 2016, 24 June 2016, 2 November 2016
Guitar Player: July 1977, January 1993
Independent: 30 April 1998, 26 November 2014
Los Angeles Times: 6 December 1988
Mojo: February 2010, October 2016
Musician: June 1990
Pop Matters: 31 October 2011

Q Magazine: December 1990
Rolling Stone: 13 March 1975, 26 November 1970, 26 September 1990, 13 December 2007
Times: 18 December 1993, 29 November 2006, 11 December 2007, 8 January 2010
Uncut: May 2005
Vanity Fair: 18 February 2014
Wall *Street Journal*: 29 May 2014

Websites (accessed August-November 2017)

45cat: www.45cat.com
Allmusic: www.allmusic.com/song/carouselambra-mt0018744412
Baroni, N., Slash names his Top 12 Guitarists of All Time. *Music Feeds*, 22 September 2014, musicfeeds.com.au/news/slash-names-his-12-best-guitarists-of-all-time/
Discogs: www.discogs.com
Drozdowski, T., Celebration Day: Jimmy Page's Top 10 Guitar Moments, 7 January 2011, www.gibson.com/News-Lifestyle/Features/en-us/jimmy-page-0107-2011.aspx
Jimmy Page tells the story of "Kashmir"'. Open Culture, 30 September 2013, www.openculture.com/2011/09/jimmy_page_tells_the_story_of_kashmir.html
Led Zeppelin discography: www.45cat.com/artist/led-zeppelin/uk
Long, A., 'Get the Led Out'. *Global Bass Online*, March 2002, www.globalbass.com/archives/mar2002/john_paul_jones.htm
Schulps, D., Interview with Jimmy Page, Trouser Press, October 1977, www.yazda.org/ipk.cgi/zh/00/http/www.iem.ac.ru/zeppelin/docs/interviews/page_77.trp
Slash names his Top 12 Guitarists of All Time. *Music Feeds*, 22 September 2014, musicfeeds.com.au/news/slash-names-his-12-best-guitarists-of-all-time/
'Stairway to Heaven' Trial: Led Zeppelin Bassist John Paul Jones Testifies for Bandmates. *Billboard,* 18 June 2016
Tight But Loose—The Led Zeppelin Magazine: www.tightbutloose.co.uk
Tolinski, B., 'Led Vault: Jimmy Page talks first three Led Zeppelin albums, Gibson and Harmony guitars and more.' *Guitar World*, June 2014, www.guitarworld.com/magazine/led-vault-jimmy-page-talks-first-three-led-zeppelin-albums-gibson-and-harmony-guitars-and-more
Tolinski, B., and Benedetto, G. Di., 'Light and Shade.' *Guitar World*, January 1998, www.guitarworld.com/features/brad-tolinskis-light-shade-conversations-jimmy-page-revelatory-portrait-led-zeppelin-guitarist
Wilkening, M., Ultimate Classic Rock: Top 40 Led Zeppelin Songs, 2013, ultimateclassicrock.com/led-zeppelin-top-50-songs/